DUMB TYPE
2022

La Biennale di Venezia
59. Esposizione Internazionale d'Arte
Partecipazioni Nazionali

ダムタイプ
2022

第59回ヴェネチア・ビエンナーレ国際美術展　日本館

2022年4月23日－11月27日
主催：国際交流基金

日本館展示　帰国展
「ダムタイプ｜2022: remap」

アーティゾン美術館
2023年2月25日－5月14日
主催：公益財団法人石橋財団アーティゾン美術館、
国際交流基金

DUMB TYPE
2022

The 59th International Art Exhibition
La Biennale di Venezia
Japan Pavilion

23 April–27 November 2022
Organizer: The Japan Foundation

Japan Pavilion Exhibition in Tokyo
DUMB TYPE, 2022: remap

Artizon Museum
25 February–14 May 2023
Organizer: Artizon Museum, Ishibashi Foundation
The Japan Foundation

目次

CONTENTS

「第59回ヴェネチア・ビエンナーレ国際美術展」に際して、国際交流基金はダムタイプによる新作インスタレーション「2022」を日本館において展示いたします。

ダムタイプは、ヴィジュアル・アート、映像、コンピューター・プログラム、音楽、ダンス、デザインなど多様な分野における、様々な世代のメンバーによって構成される日本を代表するアーティスト・コレクティヴです。35年におよぶ創作活動の中で、ダムタイプはプロジェクトごとにメンバーが入れ替わりながらも、常に社会を取り巻く環境をリアルに感じ、把握しながら、新たな表現を模索し続けています。

本作品では、ダムタイプが自作したデバイスが会場の東西南北に設置され、そこから発せられるレーザーと音が、シンプルで普遍的な問いを来場者に投げかけます。その一方で部屋の中央には何もない対蹠的な空間が存在し、インターネット／ソーシャルメディアの進化、新型コロナウイルスにより大きく変化したコミュニケーションや世界を知覚する方法、さらには「Post Truth」や「Liminal space」といった概念が重層的に表現されます。この作品が提示するのは、「2022」というタイトルが示すとおり、極めて現実的、現代的な問題意識であると言えるでしょう。是非じっくりと時間をかけて本作品と向き合っていただければ幸甚に存じます。

本展の開催にあたりまして、新作をもって臨んでくださったダムタイプに心より感謝申し上げます。また、ご支援くださいました公益財団法人石橋財団をはじめ、本展の実現に向けてお力添えをくださいましたすべての皆様方に対しまして、深甚なる謝意を表します。

国際交流基金

The Japan Foundation presents a new work by Dumb Type, *2022*, in the Japan Pavilion at the 59th International Art Exhibition of La Biennale di Venezia.

Dumb Type is a preeminent artist collective from Japan, consisting of artists of different generations and from diverse backgrounds, including visual art, video, programming, music, dance, and design. In each of its creative projects over the past thirty-five years, with membership changing from production to production, Dumb Type has consistently sensed and identified the reality of issues affecting society, and explored new forms of artistic expression to address such issues.

The installation for the Japan Pavilion incorporates devices fabricated by Dumb Type, positioned to the north, south, east, and west within the exhibition room. Projecting laser light and audio, they pose simple yet universal questions to the venue audience. In contrast to those surroundings, there is a void in the center of the room. This configuration is an expression of methods of perceiving the world and methods of communication greatly transformed under the COVID-19 pandemic and the evolution of social media, layered with the concepts of post-truth and liminal space. The title, *2022*, emphasizes the actuality and the contemporaneity of the issues addressed, and the installation rewards viewers who take the time to concentrate and slowly absorb the experience.

The Japan Foundation is grateful to Dumb Type for creating this new work for Venice. We would also like to express our deep gratitude to the Ishibashi Foundation for its support and to each of the other entities and individuals whose efforts have contributed to realizing this exhibition.

The Japan Foundation

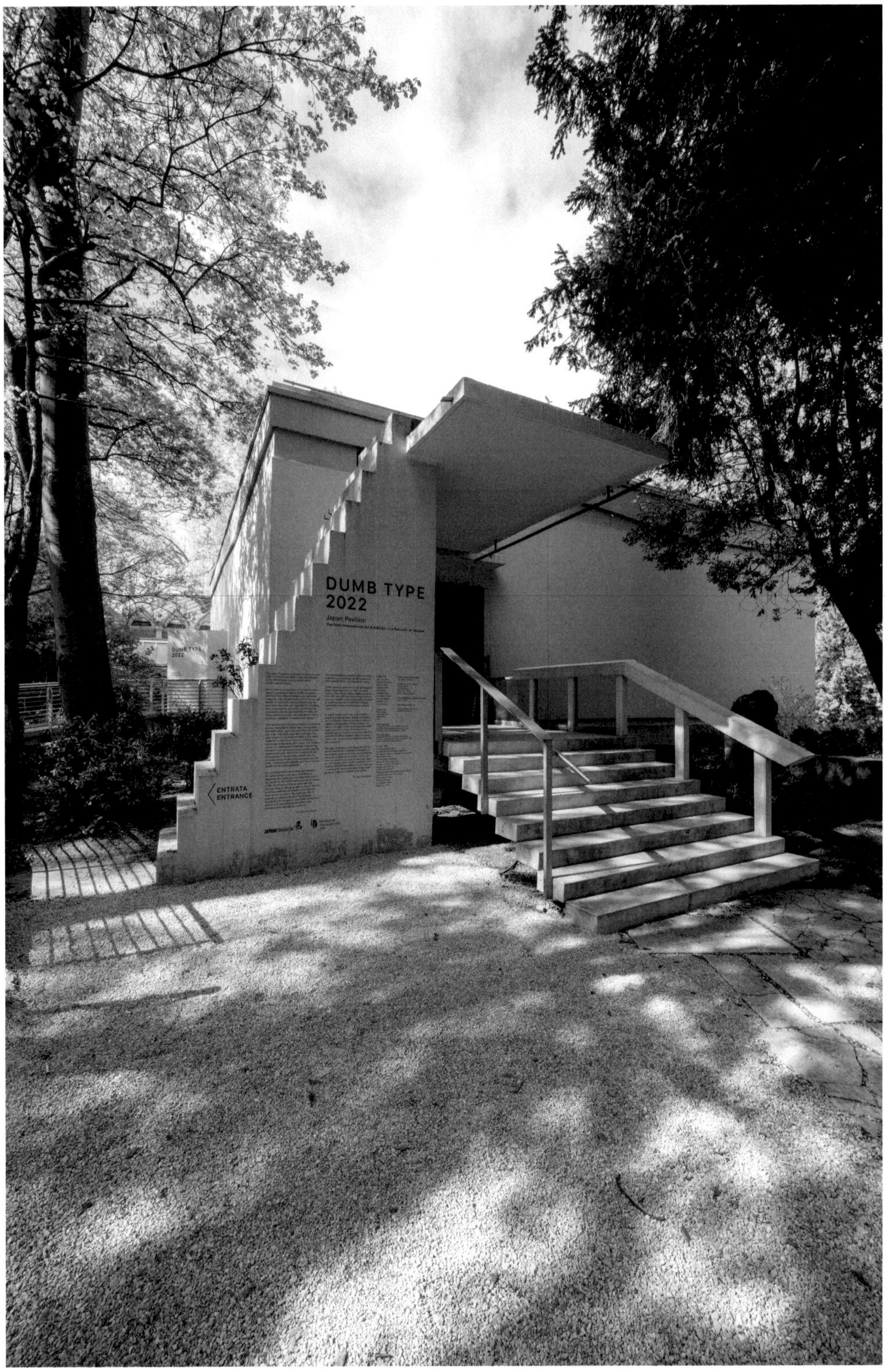
DUMB TYPE
2022
Japan Pavilion
DUMB TYPE
2022
ENTRATA
ENTRANCE

WHAT IS GEOGRAPHY? WHAT IS THE EARTH? WHAT IS THE SHAPE OF THE EARTH? OF WH
ICH CONTINENT DO WE LIVE? WHAT IS AN OCEAN? HOW MANY OCEANS ARE THERE? WHIC
T IS A VOLCANO? WHAT IS A DESERT? BY WHAT ARE DESERTS FORMED? WHAT IS A RIV
VERNS A REPUBLIC? WHICH IS THE LARGEST EMPIRE IN THE WORLD? WHICH IS THE LA
ISION OF THE EARTH DO WE LIVE? WHEN YOU LOOK AT THE RISING SUN, WHAT OCEAN
U LOOK AT THE SETTING SUN, WHAT OCEAN IS BEFORE YOU? WHERE DOES THE SUN SET
T SEA SOUTH OF EUROPE? WHICH IS THE LARGEST ISLAND IN THE WORLD? HOW MANY C
FURTHEST SOUTH? IN WHAT COUNTRY DO WE LIVE? WHERE IS CAPE FAREWELL? WHAT IS
COMPOSED? WHAT IS A CONTINENT? HOW MANY CONTINENTS ARE THERE? ON WHICH CONT
OCEAN? WHAT IS AN IS LAND? WHAT IS A MOUNTAIN? WHAT IS A HILL? WHAT IS A VO
IVERS FORMED? WHO GOVERNS AN EMPIRE? WHO GOVERNS A KINGDOM? WHO GOVERNS A R
THE WORLD? WHICH IS THE LARGEST REPUBLIC IN THE WORLD? IN WHAT DIVISION OF
ERE DOES THE SUN RISE? WHERE, THEN, IS THE ATLANTIC OCEAN? WHEN YOU LOOK AT
OF ASIA? WHAT OCEAN SOUTH OF ASIA? WHAT OCEAN WEST OF AFRICA? WHAT SEA SOUT
? HOW ARE THEY DIVIDED? WHAT COUNTRY FURTHEST NORTH? WHAT COUNTRY FURTHEST
IS THE EARTH? WHAT IS THE SHAPE OF THE EARTH? OF WHAT IS THE EARTH COMPOSED
? WHAT IS AN OCEAN? HOW MANY OCEANS ARE THERE? WHICH IS THE LARGEST OCEAN?
A DESERT? BY WHAT ARE DESERTS FORMED? WHAT IS A RIVER? BY WHAT ARE RIVERS F
IS THE LARGEST EMPIRE IN THE WORLD? WHICH IS THE LARGEST KINGDOM IN THE WOR
LIVE? WHEN YOU LOOK AT THE RISING SUN, WHAT OCEAN IS BEFORE YOU? WHERE DOES
, WHAT OCEAN IS BEFORE YOU? WHERE DOES THE SUN SET? WHAT OCEAN EAST OF ASIA
ICH IS THE LARGEST ISLAND IN THE WORLD? HOW MANY COUNTRIES ARE THERE? HOW A
COUNTRY DO WE LIVE? WHERE IS CAPE FAREWELL? WHAT IS GEOGRAPHY? WHAT IS THE
TINENT? HOW MANY CONTINENTS ARE THERE? ON WHICH CONTINENT DO WE LIVE? WHAT
AND? WHAT IS A MOUNTAIN? WHAT IS A HILL? WHAT IS A VOLCANO? WHAT IS A DESER
RNS AN EMPIRE? WHO GOVERNS A KINGDOM? WHO GOVERNS A REPUBLIC? WHICH IS THE
E LARGEST REPUBLIC IN THE WORLD? IN WHAT DIVISION OF THE EARTH DO WE LIVE?
WHERE, THEN, IS THE ATLANTIC OCEAN? WHEN YOU LOOK AT THE SETTING SUN, WHAT
UTH OF ASIA? WHAT OCEAN WEST OF AFRICA? WHAT SEA SOUTH OF EUROPE? WHICH IS
? WHAT COUNTRY FURTHEST NORTH? WHAT COUNTRY FURTHEST SOUTH? IN WHAT COUNTRY
THE SHAPE OF THE EARTH? OF WHAT IS THE EARTH COMPOSED? WHAT IS A CONTINENT?
W MANY OCEANS ARE THERE? WHICH IS THE LARGEST OCEAN? WHAT IS AN IS LAND? WH
DESERTS FORMED? WHAT IS A RIVER? BY WHAT ARE RIVERS FORMED? WHO GOVERNS AN
IN THE WORLD? WHICH IS THE LARGEST KINGDOM IN THE WORLD? WHICH IS THE LARGE
T THE RISING SUN, WHAT OCEAN IS BEFORE YOU? WHERE DOES THE SUN RISE? WHERE,
E YOU? WHERE DOES THE SUN SET? WHAT OCEAN EAST OF ASIA? WHAT OCEAN SOUTH OF
LAND IN THE WORLD? HOW MANY COUNTRIES ARE THERE? HOW ARE THEY DIVIDED? WHAT
HERE IS CAPE FAREWELL? WHAT IS GEOGRAPHY? WHAT IS THE EARTH? WHAT IS THE SH
INENTS ARE THERE? ON WHICH CONTINENT DO WE LIVE? WHAT IS AN OCEAN? HOW MANY
IN? WHAT IS A HILL? WHAT IS A VOLCANO? WHAT IS A DESERT? BY WHAT ARE DESERT
VERNS A KINGDOM? WHO GOVERNS A REPUBLIC? WHICH IS THE LARGEST EMPIRE IN THE
THE WORLD? IN WHAT DIVISION OF THE EARTH DO WE LIVE? WHEN YOU LOOK AT THE R
TLANTIC OCEAN? WHEN YOU LOOK AT THE SETTING SUN, WHAT OCEAN IS BEFORE YOU?
AN WEST OF AFRICA? WHAT SEA SOUTH OF EUROPE? WHICH IS THE LARGEST ISLAND IN
ST NORTH? WHAT COUNTRY FURTHEST SOUTH? IN WHAT COUNTRY DO WE LIVE? WHERE IS
H? OF WHAT IS THE EARTH COMPOSED? WHAT IS A CONTINENT? HOW MANY CONTINENTS
RE? WHICH IS THE LARGEST OCEAN? WHAT IS AN IS LAND? WHAT IS A MOUNTAIN? WHA
IS A RIVER? BY WHAT ARE RIVERS FORMED? WHO GOVERNS AN EMPIRE? WHO GOVERNS A
S THE LARGEST KINGDOM IN THE WORLD? WHICH IS THE LARGEST REPUBLIC IN THE WO
T OCEAN IS BEFORE YOU? WHERE DOES THE SUN RISE? WHERE, THEN, IS THE ATLANTI
SUN SET? WHAT OCEAN EAST OF ASIA? WHAT OCEAN SOUTH OF ASIA? WHAT OCEAN WEST
MANY COUNTRIES ARE THERE? HOW ARE THEY DIVIDED? WHAT COUNTRY FURTHEST NORTH
WHAT IS GEOGRAPHY? WHAT IS THE EARTH? WHAT IS THE SHAPE OF THE EARTH? OF WH
ICH CONTINENT DO WE LIVE? WHAT IS AN OCEAN? HOW MANY OCEANS ARE THERE? WHIC
T IS A VOLCANO? WHAT IS A DESERT? BY WHAT ARE DESERTS FORMED? WHAT IS A RIV
VERNS A REPUBLIC? WHICH IS THE LARGEST EMPIRE IN THE WORLD? WHICH IS THE LA
[illegible]
U LOOK AT THE SETTING SUN, WHAT OCEAN IS BEFORE YOU? WHERE DOES THE SUN SET
T SEA SOUTH OF EUROPE? WHICH IS THE LARGEST ISLAND IN THE WORLD? HOW MANY C
FURTHEST SOUTH? IN WHAT COUNTRY DO WE LIVE? WHERE IS CAPE FAREWELL? WHAT IS
COMPOSED? WHAT IS A CONTINENT? HOW MANY CONTINENTS ARE THERE? ON WHICH CONT
OCEAN? WHAT IS AN IS LAND? WHAT IS A MOUNTAIN? WHAT IS A HILL? WHAT IS A VO
IVERS FORMED? WHO GOVERNS AN EMPIRE? WHO GOVERNS A KINGDOM? WHO GOVERNS A R
THE WORLD? WHICH IS THE LARGEST REPUBLIC IN THE WORLD? IN WHAT DIVISION OF
ERE DOES THE SUN RISE? WHERE, THEN, IS THE ATLANTIC OCEAN? WHEN YOU LOOK AT
OF ASIA? WHAT OCEAN SOUTH OF ASIA? WHAT OCEAN WEST OF AFRICA? WHAT SEA SOUT
? HOW ARE THEY DIVIDED? WHAT COUNTRY FURTHEST NORTH? WHAT COUNTRY FURTHEST
IS THE EARTH? WHAT IS THE SHAPE OF THE EARTH? OF WHAT IS THE EARTH COMPOSED
? WHAT IS AN OCEAN? HOW MANY OCEANS ARE THERE? WHICH IS THE LARGEST OCEAN?
A DESERT? BY WHAT ARE DESERTS FORMED? WHAT IS A RIVER? BY WHAT ARE RIVERS F
IS THE LARGEST EMPIRE IN THE WORLD? WHICH IS THE LARGEST KINGDOM IN THE WOR
LIVE? WHEN YOU LOOK AT THE RISING SUN, WHAT OCEAN IS BEFORE YOU? WHERE DOES
, WHAT OCEAN IS BEFORE YOU? WHERE DOES THE SUN SET? WHAT OCEAN EAST OF ASIA
ICH IS THE LARGEST ISLAND IN THE WORLD? HOW MANY COUNTRIES ARE THERE? HOW A
COUNTRY DO WE LIVE? WHERE IS CAPE FAREWELL? WHAT IS GEOGRAPHY? WHAT IS THE
TINENT? HOW MANY CONTINENTS ARE THERE? ON WHICH CONTINENT DO WE LIVE? WHAT
AND? WHAT IS A MOUNTAIN? WHAT IS A HILL? WHAT IS A VOLCANO? WHAT IS A DESER
RNS AN EMPIRE? WHO GOVERNS A KINGDOM? WHO GOVERNS A REPUBLIC? WHICH IS THE
E LARGEST REPUBLIC IN THE WORLD? IN WHAT DIVISION OF THE EARTH DO WE LIVE?
WHERE, THEN, IS THE ATLANTIC OCEAN? WHEN YOU LOOK AT THE SETTING SUN, WHAT
UTH OF ASIA? WHAT OCEAN WEST OF AFRICA? WHAT SEA SOUTH OF EUROPE? WHICH IS
? WHAT COUNTRY FURTHEST NORTH? WHAT COUNTRY FURTHEST SOUTH? IN WHAT COUNTRY
THE SHAPE OF THE EARTH? OF WHAT IS THE EARTH COMPOSED? WHAT IS A CONTINENT?
W MANY OCEANS ARE THERE? WHICH IS THE LARGEST OCEAN? WHAT IS AN IS LAND? WH
DESERTS FORMED? WHAT IS A RIVER? BY WHAT ARE RIVERS FORMED? WHO GOVERNS AN
IN THE WORLD? WHICH IS THE LARGEST KINGDOM IN THE WORLD? WHICH IS THE LARGE
T THE RISING SUN, WHAT OCEAN IS BEFORE YOU? WHERE DOES THE SUN RISE? WHERE,
E YOU? WHERE DOES THE SUN SET? WHAT OCEAN EAST OF ASIA? WHAT OCEAN SOUTH OF
LAND IN THE WORLD? HOW MANY COUNTRIES ARE THERE? HOW ARE THEY DIVIDED? WHAT
HERE IS CAPE FAREWELL? WHAT IS GEOGRAPHY? WHAT IS THE EARTH? WHAT IS THE SH
INENTS ARE THERE? ON WHICH CONTINENT DO WE LIVE? WHAT IS AN OCEAN? HOW MANY
IN? WHAT IS A HILL? WHAT IS A VOLCANO? WHAT IS A DESERT? BY WHAT ARE DESERT
VERNS A KINGDOM? WHO GOVERNS A REPUBLIC? WHICH IS THE LARGEST EMPIRE IN THE
THE WORLD? IN WHAT DIVISION OF THE EARTH DO WE LIVE? WHEN YOU LOOK AT THE R
TLANTIC OCEAN? WHEN YOU LOOK AT THE SETTING SUN, WHAT OCEAN IS BEFORE YOU?
AN WEST OF AFRICA? WHAT SEA SOUTH OF EUROPE? WHICH IS THE LARGEST ISLAND IN
ST NORTH? WHAT COUNTRY FURTHEST SOUTH? IN WHAT COUNTRY DO WE LIVE? WHERE IS
H? OF WHAT IS THE EARTH COMPOSED? WHAT IS A CONTINENT? HOW MANY CONTINENTS
RE? WHICH IS THE LARGEST OCEAN? WHAT IS AN IS LAND? WHAT IS A MOUNTAIN? WHA
IS A RIVER? BY WHAT ARE RIVERS FORMED? WHO GOVERNS AN EMPIRE? WHO GOVERNS A
S THE LARGEST KINGDOM IN THE WORLD? WHICH IS THE LARGEST REPUBLIC IN THE WO
T OCEAN IS BEFORE YOU? WHERE DOES THE SUN RISE? WHERE, THEN, IS THE ATLANTI
SUN SET? WHAT OCEAN EAST OF ASIA? WHAT OCEAN SOUTH OF ASIA? WHAT OCEAN WEST
MANY COUNTRIES ARE THERE? HOW ARE THEY DIVIDED? WHAT COUNTRY FURTHEST NORTH
WHAT IS GEOGRAPHY? WHAT IS THE EARTH? WHAT IS THE SHAPE OF THE EARTH? OF WH
ICH CONTINENT DO WE LIVE? WHAT IS AN OCEAN? HOW MANY OCEANS ARE THERE? WHIC
T IS A VOLCANO? WHAT IS A DESERT? BY WHAT ARE DESERTS FORMED? WHAT IS A RIV
VERNS A REPUBLIC? WHICH IS THE LARGEST EMPIRE IN THE WORLD? WHICH IS THE LA
ISION OF THE EARTH DO WE LIVE? WHEN YOU LOOK AT THE RISING SUN, WHAT OCEAN
U LOOK AT THE SETTING SUN, WHAT OCEAN IS BEFORE YOU? WHERE DOES THE SUN SET
T SEA SOUTH OF EUROPE? WHICH IS THE LARGEST ISLAND IN THE WORLD? HOW MANY C
FURTHEST SOUTH? IN WHAT COUNTRY DO WE LIVE? WHERE IS CAPE FAREWELL? WHAT IS
COMPOSED? WHAT IS A CONTINENT? HOW MANY CONTINENTS ARE THERE? ON WHICH CONT
OCEAN? WHAT IS AN IS LAND? WHAT IS A MOUNTAIN? WHAT IS A HILL? WHAT IS A VO
IVERS FORMED? WHO GOVERNS AN EMPIRE? WHO GOVERNS A KINGDOM? WHO GOVERNS A R
THE WORLD? WHICH IS THE LARGEST REPUBLIC IN THE WORLD? IN WHAT DIVISION OF
ERE DOES THE SUN RISE? WHERE, THEN, IS THE ATLANTIC OCEAN? WHEN YOU LOOK AT
OF ASIA? WHAT OCEAN SOUTH OF ASIA? WHAT OCEAN WEST OF AFRICA? WHAT SEA SOUT

E EARTH COMPOSED? WHAT IS A CONTINENT? HOW MANY CONTINENTS ARE THERE? ON WH
LARGEST OCEAN? WHAT IS AN IS LAND? WHAT IS A MOUNTAIN? WHAT IS A HILL? WHA
HAT ARE RIVERS FORMED? WHO GOVERNS AN EMPIRE? WHO GOVERNS A KINGDOM? WHO GO
NGDOM IN THE WORLD? WHICH IS THE LARGEST REPUBLIC IN THE WORLD? IN WHAT DIV
E YOU? WHERE DOES THE SUN RISE? WHERE, THEN, IS THE ATLANTIC OCEAN? WHEN YO
CEAN EAST OF ASIA? WHAT OCEAN SOUTH OF ASIA? WHAT OCEAN WEST OF AFRICA? WHA
ARE THERE? HOW ARE THEY DIVIDED? WHAT COUNTRY FURTHEST NORTH? WHAT COUNTRY
HY? WHAT IS THE EARTH? WHAT IS THE SHAPE OF THE EARTH? OF WHAT IS THE EARTH
WE LIVE? WHAT IS AN OCEAN? HOW MANY OCEANS ARE THERE? WHICH IS THE LARGEST
HAT IS A DESERT? BY WHAT ARE DESERTS FORMED? WHAT IS A RIVER? BY WHAT ARE R
WHICH IS THE LARGEST EMPIRE IN THE WORLD? WHICH IS THE LARGEST KINGDOM IN
H DO WE LIVE? WHEN YOU LOOK AT THE RISING SUN, WHAT OCEAN IS BEFORE YOU? WH
TING SUN, WHAT OCEAN IS BEFORE YOU? WHERE DOES THE SUN SET? WHAT OCEAN EAST
OPE? WHICH IS THE LARGEST ISLAND IN THE WORLD? HOW MANY COUNTRIES ARE THERE
N WHAT COUNTRY DO WE LIVE? WHERE IS CAPE FAREWELL? WHAT IS GEOGRAPHY? WHAT
S A CONTINENT? HOW MANY CONTINENTS ARE THERE? ON WHICH CONTINENT DO WE LIVE
AN IS LAND? WHAT IS A MOUNTAIN? WHAT IS A HILL? WHAT IS A VOLCANO? WHAT IS
HO GOVERNS AN EMPIRE? WHO GOVERNS A KINGDOM? WHO GOVERNS A REPUBLIC? WHICH
H IS THE LARGEST REPUBLIC IN THE WORLD? IN WHAT DIVISION OF THE EARTH DO WE
RISE? WHERE, THEN, IS THE ATLANTIC OCEAN? WHEN YOU LOOK AT THE SETTING SUN
CEAN SOUTH OF ASIA? WHAT OCEAN WEST OF AFRICA? WHAT SEA SOUTH OF EUROPE? WH
DIVIDED? WHAT COUNTRY FURTHEST NORTH? WHAT COUNTRY FURTHEST SOUTH? IN WHAT
HAT IS THE SHAPE OF THE EARTH? OF WHAT IS THE EARTH COMPOSED? WHAT IS A CON
EAN? HOW MANY OCEANS ARE THERE? WHICH IS THE LARGEST OCEAN? WHAT IS AN IS L
AT ARE DESERTS FORMED? WHAT IS A RIVER? BY WHAT ARE RIVERS FORMED? WHO GOVE
EMPIRE IN THE WORLD? WHICH IS THE LARGEST KINGDOM IN THE WORLD? WHICH IS TH
LOOK AT THE RISING SUN, WHAT OCEAN IS BEFORE YOU? WHERE DOES THE SUN RISE?
BEFORE YOU? WHERE DOES THE SUN SET? WHAT OCEAN EAST OF ASIA? WHAT OCEAN SO
EST ISLAND IN THE WORLD? HOW MANY COUNTRIES ARE THERE? HOW ARE THEY DIVIDED
IVE? WHERE IS CAPE FAREWELL? WHAT IS GEOGRAPHY? WHAT IS THE EARTH? WHAT IS
Y CONTINENTS ARE THERE? ON WHICH CONTINENT DO WE LIVE? WHAT IS AN OCEAN? HO
MOUNTAIN? WHAT IS A HILL? WHAT IS A VOLCANO? WHAT IS A DESERT? BY WHAT ARE
WHO GOVERNS A KINGDOM? WHO GOVERNS A REPUBLIC? WHICH IS THE LARGEST EMPIRE
LIC IN THE WORLD? IN WHAT DIVISION OF THE EARTH DO WE LIVE? WHEN YOU LOOK A
S THE ATLANTIC OCEAN? WHEN YOU LOOK AT THE SETTING SUN, WHAT OCEAN IS BEFOR
HAT OCEAN WEST OF AFRICA? WHAT SEA SOUTH OF EUROPE? WHICH IS THE LARGEST IS
FURTHEST NORTH? WHAT COUNTRY FURTHEST SOUTH? IN WHAT COUNTRY DO WE LIVE? W
HE EARTH? OF WHAT IS THE EARTH COMPOSED? WHAT IS A CONTINENT? HOW MANY CONT
ARE THERE? WHICH IS THE LARGEST OCEAN? WHAT IS AN IS LAND? WHAT IS A MOUNTA
? WHAT IS A RIVER? BY WHAT ARE RIVERS FORMED? WHO GOVERNS AN EMPIRE? WHO GO
WHICH IS THE LARGEST KINGDOM IN THE WORLD? WHICH IS THE LARGEST REPUBLIC IN
N, WHAT OCEAN IS BEFORE YOU? WHERE DOES THE SUN RISE? WHERE, THEN, IS THE A
ES THE SUN SET? WHAT OCEAN EAST OF ASIA? WHAT OCEAN SOUTH OF ASIA? WHAT OCE
LD? HOW MANY COUNTRIES ARE THERE? HOW ARE THEY DIVIDED? WHAT COUNTRY FURTHE
REWELL? WHAT IS GEOGRAPHY? WHAT IS THE EARTH? WHAT IS THE SHAPE OF THE EART
E? ON WHICH CONTINENT DO WE LIVE? WHAT IS AN OCEAN? HOW MANY OCEANS ARE THE
ILL? WHAT IS A VOLCANO? WHAT IS A DESERT? BY WHAT ARE DESERTS FORMED? WHAT
? WHO GOVERNS A REPUBLIC? WHICH IS THE LARGEST EMPIRE IN THE WORLD? WHICH I
WHAT DIVISION OF THE EARTH DO WE LIVE? WHEN YOU LOOK AT THE RISING SUN, WHA
WHEN YOU LOOK AT THE SETTING SUN, WHAT OCEAN IS BEFORE YOU? WHERE DOES THE
CA? WHAT SEA SOUTH OF EUROPE? WHICH IS THE LARGEST ISLAND IN THE WORLD? HOW
OUNTRY FURTHEST SOUTH? IN WHAT COUNTRY DO WE LIVE? WHERE IS CAPE FAREWELL?
E EARTH COMPOSED? WHAT IS A CONTINENT? HOW MANY CONTINENTS ARE THERE? ON WH
LARGEST OCEAN? WHAT IS AN IS LAND? WHAT IS A MOUNTAIN? WHAT IS A HILL? WHA
HAT ARE RIVERS FORMED? WHO GOVERNS AN EMPIRE? WHO GOVERNS A KINGDOM? WHO GO
NGDOM IN THE WORLD? WHICH IS THE LARGEST REPUBLIC IN THE WORLD? IN WHAT DIV
[illegible]
CEAN EAST OF ASIA? WHAT OCEAN SOUTH OF ASIA? WHAT OCEAN WEST OF AFRICA? WHA
ARE THERE? HOW ARE THEY DIVIDED? WHAT COUNTRY FURTHEST NORTH? WHAT COUNTRY
HY? WHAT IS THE EARTH? WHAT IS THE SHAPE OF THE EARTH? OF WHAT IS THE EARTH
WE LIVE? WHAT IS AN OCEAN? HOW MANY OCEANS ARE THERE? WHICH IS THE LARGEST
HAT IS A DESERT? BY WHAT ARE DESERTS FORMED? WHAT IS A RIVER? BY WHAT ARE R
WHICH IS THE LARGEST EMPIRE IN THE WORLD? WHICH IS THE LARGEST KINGDOM IN
H DO WE LIVE? WHEN YOU LOOK AT THE RISING SUN, WHAT OCEAN IS BEFORE YOU? WH
TING SUN, WHAT OCEAN IS BEFORE YOU? WHERE DOES THE SUN SET? WHAT OCEAN EAST
OPE? WHICH IS THE LARGEST ISLAND IN THE WORLD? HOW MANY COUNTRIES ARE THERE
N WHAT COUNTRY DO WE LIVE? WHERE IS CAPE FAREWELL? WHAT IS GEOGRAPHY? WHAT
S A CONTINENT? HOW MANY CONTINENTS ARE THERE? ON WHICH CONTINENT DO WE LIVE
AN IS LAND? WHAT IS A MOUNTAIN? WHAT IS A HILL? WHAT IS A VOLCANO? WHAT IS
HO GOVERNS AN EMPIRE? WHO GOVERNS A KINGDOM? WHO GOVERNS A REPUBLIC? WHICH
H IS THE LARGEST REPUBLIC IN THE WORLD? IN WHAT DIVISION OF THE EARTH DO WE
RISE? WHERE, THEN, IS THE ATLANTIC OCEAN? WHEN YOU LOOK AT THE SETTING SUN
CEAN SOUTH OF ASIA? WHAT OCEAN WEST OF AFRICA? WHAT SEA SOUTH OF EUROPE? WH
DIVIDED? WHAT COUNTRY FURTHEST NORTH? WHAT COUNTRY FURTHEST SOUTH? IN WHAT
HAT IS THE SHAPE OF THE EARTH? OF WHAT IS THE EARTH COMPOSED? WHAT IS A CON
EAN? HOW MANY OCEANS ARE THERE? WHICH IS THE LARGEST OCEAN? WHAT IS AN IS L
AT ARE DESERTS FORMED? WHAT IS A RIVER? BY WHAT ARE RIVERS FORMED? WHO GOVE
EMPIRE IN THE WORLD? WHICH IS THE LARGEST KINGDOM IN THE WORLD? WHICH IS TH
LOOK AT THE RISING SUN, WHAT OCEAN IS BEFORE YOU? WHERE DOES THE SUN RISE?
BEFORE YOU? WHERE DOES THE SUN SET? WHAT OCEAN EAST OF ASIA? WHAT OCEAN SO
EST ISLAND IN THE WORLD? HOW MANY COUNTRIES ARE THERE? HOW ARE THEY DIVIDED
IVE? WHERE IS CAPE FAREWELL? WHAT IS GEOGRAPHY? WHAT IS THE EARTH? WHAT IS
Y CONTINENTS ARE THERE? ON WHICH CONTINENT DO WE LIVE? WHAT IS AN OCEAN? HO
MOUNTAIN? WHAT IS A HILL? WHAT IS A VOLCANO? WHAT IS A DESERT? BY WHAT ARE
WHO GOVERNS A KINGDOM? WHO GOVERNS A REPUBLIC? WHICH IS THE LARGEST EMPIRE
LIC IN THE WORLD? IN WHAT DIVISION OF THE EARTH DO WE LIVE? WHEN YOU LOOK A
S THE ATLANTIC OCEAN? WHEN YOU LOOK AT THE SETTING SUN, WHAT OCEAN IS BEFOR
HAT OCEAN WEST OF AFRICA? WHAT SEA SOUTH OF EUROPE? WHICH IS THE LARGEST IS
FURTHEST NORTH? WHAT COUNTRY FURTHEST SOUTH? IN WHAT COUNTRY DO WE LIVE? W
HE EARTH? OF WHAT IS THE EARTH COMPOSED? WHAT IS A CONTINENT? HOW MANY CONT
ARE THERE? WHICH IS THE LARGEST OCEAN? WHAT IS AN IS LAND? WHAT IS A MOUNTA
? WHAT IS A RIVER? BY WHAT ARE RIVERS FORMED? WHO GOVERNS AN EMPIRE? WHO GO
WHICH IS THE LARGEST KINGDOM IN THE WORLD? WHICH IS THE LARGEST REPUBLIC IN
N, WHAT OCEAN IS BEFORE YOU? WHERE DOES THE SUN RISE? WHERE, THEN, IS THE A
ES THE SUN SET? WHAT OCEAN EAST OF ASIA? WHAT OCEAN SOUTH OF ASIA? WHAT OCE
LD? HOW MANY COUNTRIES ARE THERE? HOW ARE THEY DIVIDED? WHAT COUNTRY FURTHE
REWELL? WHAT IS GEOGRAPHY? WHAT IS THE EARTH? WHAT IS THE SHAPE OF THE EART
E? ON WHICH CONTINENT DO WE LIVE? WHAT IS AN OCEAN? HOW MANY OCEANS ARE THE
ILL? WHAT IS A VOLCANO? WHAT IS A DESERT? BY WHAT ARE DESERTS FORMED? WHAT
? WHO GOVERNS A REPUBLIC? WHICH IS THE LARGEST EMPIRE IN THE WORLD? WHICH I
WHAT DIVISION OF THE EARTH DO WE LIVE? WHEN YOU LOOK AT THE RISING SUN, WHA
WHEN YOU LOOK AT THE SETTING SUN, WHAT OCEAN IS BEFORE YOU? WHERE DOES THE
CA? WHAT SEA SOUTH OF EUROPE? WHICH IS THE LARGEST ISLAND IN THE WORLD? HOW
OUNTRY FURTHEST SOUTH? IN WHAT COUNTRY DO WE LIVE? WHERE IS CAPE FAREWELL?
E EARTH COMPOSED? WHAT IS A CONTINENT? HOW MANY CONTINENTS ARE THERE? ON WH
LARGEST OCEAN? WHAT IS AN IS LAND? WHAT IS A MOUNTAIN? WHAT IS A HILL? WHA
HAT ARE RIVERS FORMED? WHO GOVERNS AN EMPIRE? WHO GOVERNS A KINGDOM? WHO GO
NGDOM IN THE WORLD? WHICH IS THE LARGEST REPUBLIC IN THE WORLD? IN WHAT DIV
E YOU? WHERE DOES THE SUN RISE? WHERE, THEN, IS THE ATLANTIC OCEAN? WHEN YO
CEAN EAST OF ASIA? WHAT OCEAN SOUTH OF ASIA? WHAT OCEAN WEST OF AFRICA? WHA
ARE THERE? HOW ARE THEY DIVIDED? WHAT COUNTRY FURTHEST NORTH? WHAT COUNTRY
HY? WHAT IS THE EARTH? WHAT IS THE SHAPE OF THE EARTH? OF WHAT IS THE EARTH
WE LIVE? WHAT IS AN OCEAN? HOW MANY OCEANS ARE THERE? WHICH IS THE LARGEST
HAT IS A DESERT? BY WHAT ARE DESERTS FORMED? WHAT IS A RIVER? BY WHAT ARE R
WHICH IS THE LARGEST EMPIRE IN THE WORLD? WHICH IS THE LARGEST KINGDOM IN
H DO WE LIVE? WHEN YOU LOOK AT THE RISING SUN, WHAT OCEAN IS BEFORE YOU? WH
TING SUN, WHAT OCEAN IS BEFORE YOU? WHERE DOES THE SUN SET? WHAT OCEAN EAST
OPE? WHICH IS THE LARGEST ISLAND IN THE WORLD? HOW MANY COUNTRIES ARE THERE

2022

展示室の中心から北・東・南・西の方角に置かれた4台の高速で回転する鏡にレーザー光を反射させて四方の壁に投影したテキストと、回転する超指向性スピーカーから流れる音声が、見えるか見えないか聴こえるか聴こえないかの境界上で、1850年代の地理の教科書から引用したシンプルで普遍的な問いを投げかける。

地球とは何ですか?
地球はどのような形ですか?
地球は何でできていますか?
大陸とは何ですか?
大陸はいくつありますか?
私たちはどの大陸に住んでいますか?
海とは何ですか?
島とは何ですか?
山とは何ですか?
火山とは何ですか?
帝国を統治するのは誰ですか?
王国を統治するのは誰ですか?
共和国を統治するのは誰ですか?
世界で一番大きい帝国はどれですか?
世界で一番大きい王国はどれですか?
世界で一番大きい共和国はどれですか?
私たちは地球のどの区域に住んでいますか?
太陽が昇る時、目の前にある海は何ですか?
太陽が沈む時、目の前にある海は何ですか?
世界で一番大きな島は何ですか?
国はいくつありますか?
それらはどのように分割されていますか?
一番北にある国は何ですか?
一番南にある国は何ですか?
私たちはどの国に住んでいますか?
ケープフェアウェル(さよなら岬)はどこにありますか?

新型コロナウイルスの影響で大きく変化した、人々のコミュニケーションの方法や世界を知覚する方法について。インターネットやソーシャルメディアによって大きく変化した、人々のコミュニケーションの方法や世界を知覚する方法について。「liminal spaces」、境界空間、光や音を感知できるかどうかの境目の領域について。

「Post Truth」、間違った情報、様々なバイアス、昔から存在するこうした事象は、拡大するソーシャルメディアの一般化によって、これまでとは全く違うステージへと移行した。進むべき方向を見定めるための灯台は、今は無数に乱立し無効になり、中心を見出せない世界の淵に立っている。その曖昧なエッジを、バランスを取りながら生きて行くことが求められている。

周囲を取り囲む言説群と対比的に、部屋の中央には空所(空虚で無効「Void」な場所)があり、それは、どこでもない場所であり、どこでもある場所である。

Mirrors on four stands positioned to the north, south, east, and west of the center of the exhibition room rotate at high speed, reflecting lasers trained on them to project text onto the surrounding walls. The projected texts are all taken from an 1850s geography textbook, posing simple yet universal questions:

What is the Earth?
What is the shape of the Earth?
Of what is the Earth composed?
What is a Continent?
How many Continents are there?
On which Continent do we live?
What is an Ocean?
What is an Island?
What is a Mountain?
What is a Volcano?
Who governs an Empire?
Who governs a Kingdom?
Who governs a Republic?
Which is the largest Empire in the world?
Which is the largest Kingdom in the world?
Which is the largest Republic in the world?
In what Division of the Earth do we live?
When you look at the rising Sun, what Ocean is before you?
When you look at the setting Sun, what Ocean is before you?
Which is the largest Island in the World?
How many Countries are there?
How are they divided?
What Country furthest north?
What Country furthest south?
In what Country do we live?
Where is Cape Farewell?

The sounds of voices reading the texts are emitted from rotating parametric speakers, becoming highly directional beams of sound that travel around the room, suddenly and unexpectedly reaching visitors' ears.

This work relates to the massive transformation in the ways in which people communicate and the ways in which we perceive the world, a transformation brought about by the evolution and growth of the internet and social media, and by the global pandemic.

In contrast to the discourses that surround it, the center of the room is an empty space—a place that exists nowhere, but at the same time a place that could be anywhere. We live in a time of post-truth and liminal spaces. The center is void.

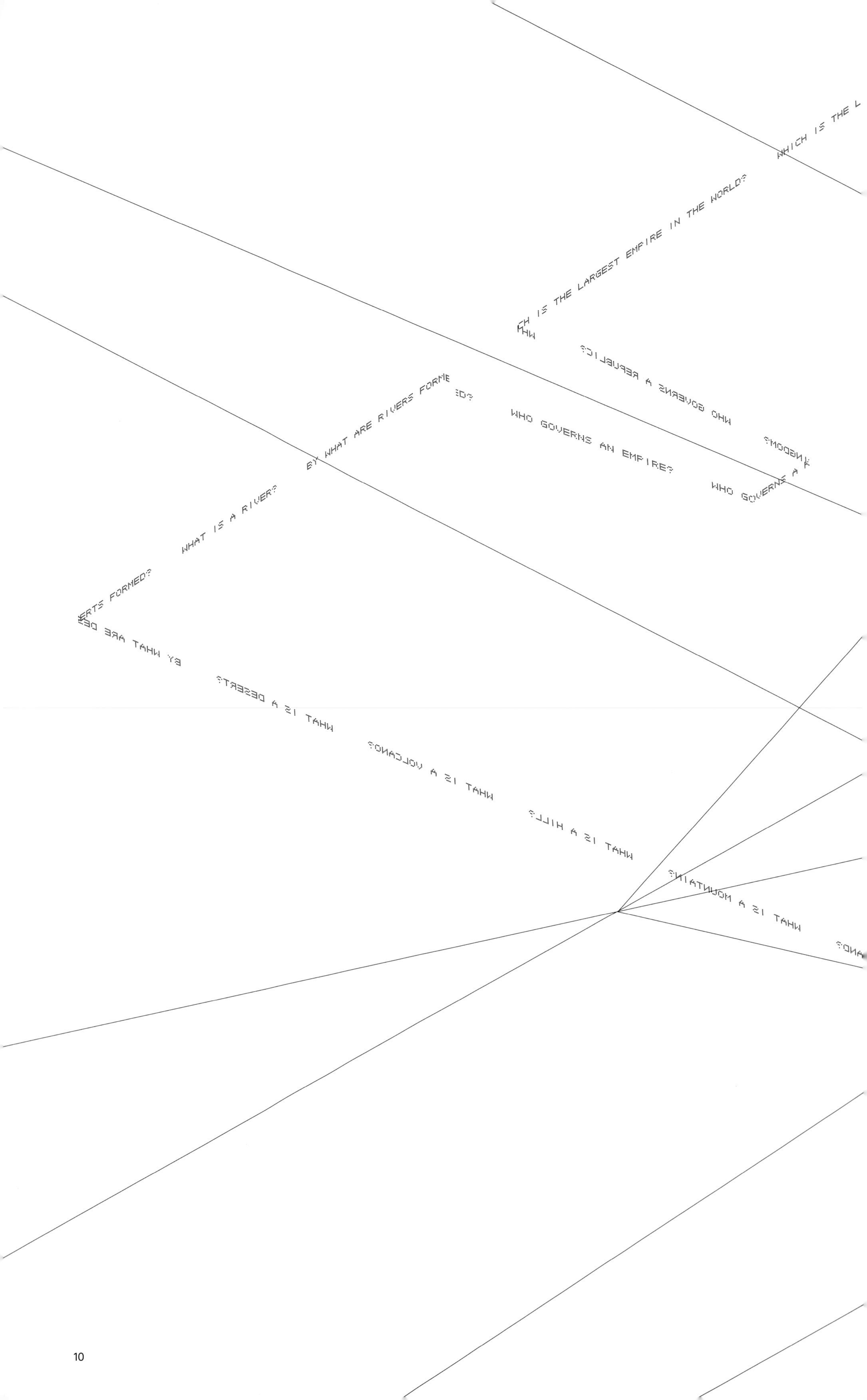
WHICH IS THE L
CH IS THE LARGEST EMPIRE IN THE WORLD?
WH
WHO GOVERNS A REPUBLIC?
BY WHAT ARE RIVERS FORMED?
WHO GOVERNS AN EMPIRE?
WHO GOVERNS A KINGDOM?
WHAT IS A RIVER?
ERTS FORMED?
BY WHAT ARE DES
WHAT IS A DESERT?
WHAT IS A VOLCANO?
WHAT IS A HILL?
WHAT IS A MOUNTAIN?
ANO?

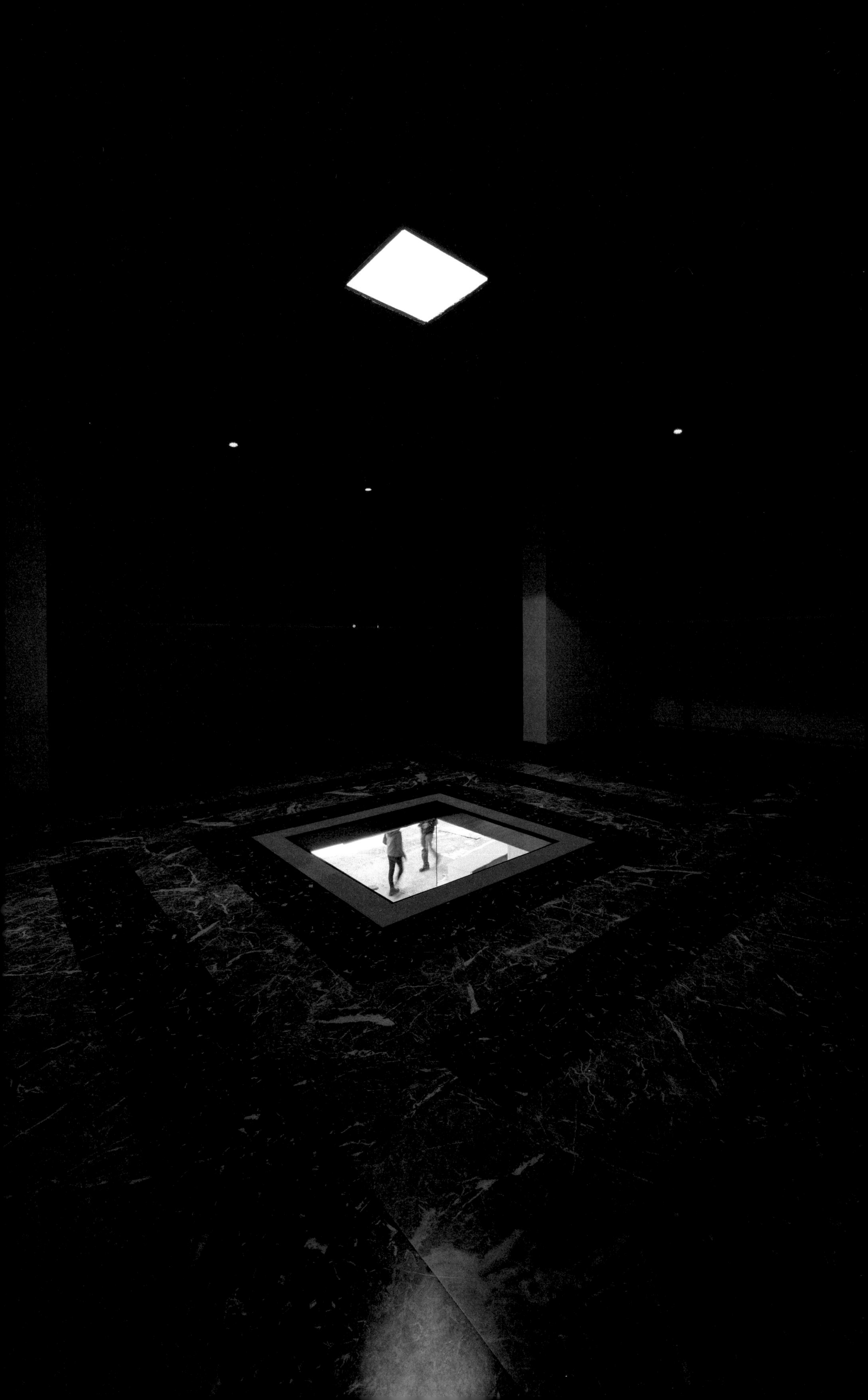

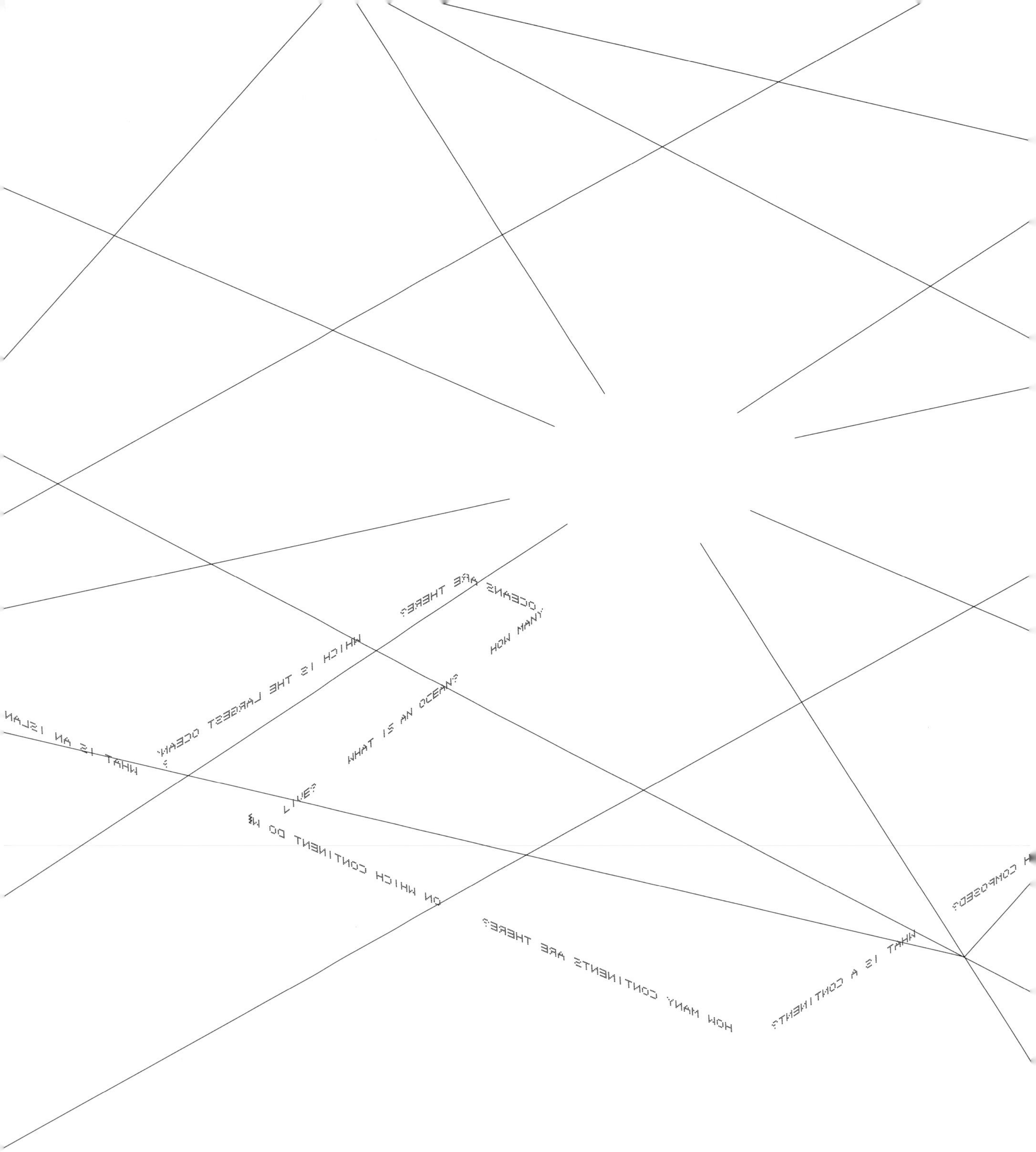

HOW MANY OCEANS ARE THERE?
WHICH IS THE LARGEST OCEAN?
WHAT IS AN OCEAN?
WHAT IS AN ISLAN
ON WHICH CONTINENT DO WE LIVE?
HOW MANY CONTINENTS ARE THERE?
WHAT IS A CONTINENT?
H COMPOSED?

T DIVISION OF THE EARTH DO WE LIVE?

WHEN, YOU LOOK AT THE RISING SUN, WHAT OCEAN IS BEFORE YOU?

WHERE DOES THE SUN RISE?

WHERE, THEN, IS THE ATLANTIC OCEAN?

WHEN YOU LOOK AT THE SETTING SUN

WHAT SEA SOUTH OF EUROPE?

WEST OF AFRICA?

WHAT IS GEOGRAPHY?

WHAT IS THE EARTH?

WHAT IS THE SHAPE OF THE EARTH?

OF WHAT IS THE EARTH COMPOSED?

WHAT IS

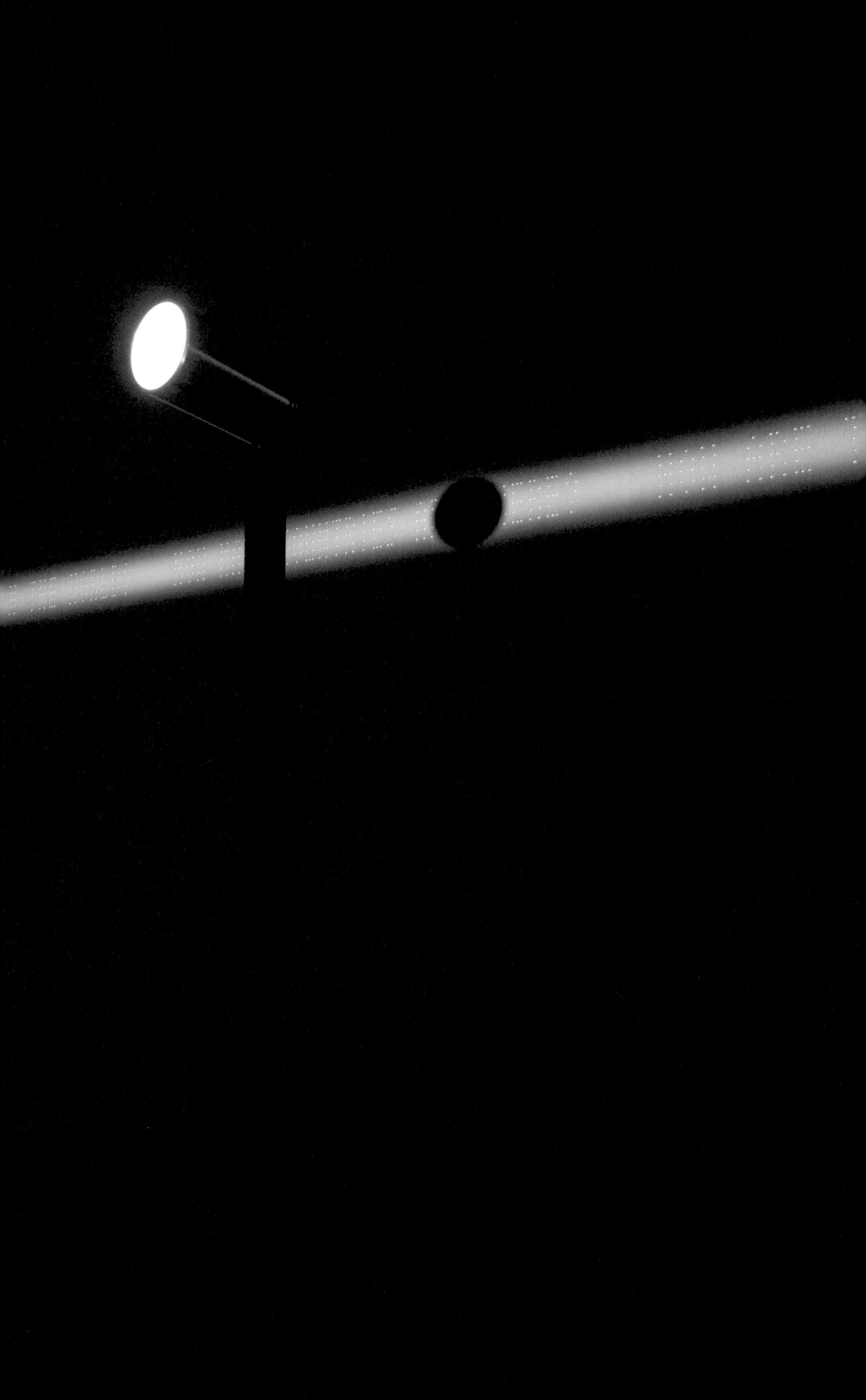

What is Geography?
What is the Earth?
What is the shape of the Earth?
Of what is the Earth composed?
What is a Continent?
How many Continents are there?
On which Continent do we live?
What is an Ocean?
How many Oceans are there?
Which is the largest Ocean?
What is an Island?
What is a Mountain?
What is a Hill?
What is a Volcano?
What is a Desert?
By what are Deserts formed?
What is a River?
By what are Rivers formed?
Who governs an Empire?
Who governs a Kingdom?
Who governs a Republic?
Which is the largest Empire in the world?
Which is the largest Kingdom in the world?
Which is the largest Republic in the world?
In what Division of the Earth do we live?
When you look at the rising Sun, what Ocean is before you?
Where does the Sun rise?
Where, then, is the Atlantic Ocean?
When you look at the setting Sun, what Ocean is before you?
Where does the Sun set?
What Ocean east of Asia?
What Ocean south of Asia?
What Ocean west of Africa?
What Sea south of Europe?
Which is the largest Island in the World?
How many Countries are there?
How are they divided?
What Country furthest north?
What Country furthest south?
In what Country do we live?
Where is Cape Farewell?

Excerpt from *First Lessons In Geography*, by James Monteith 1856

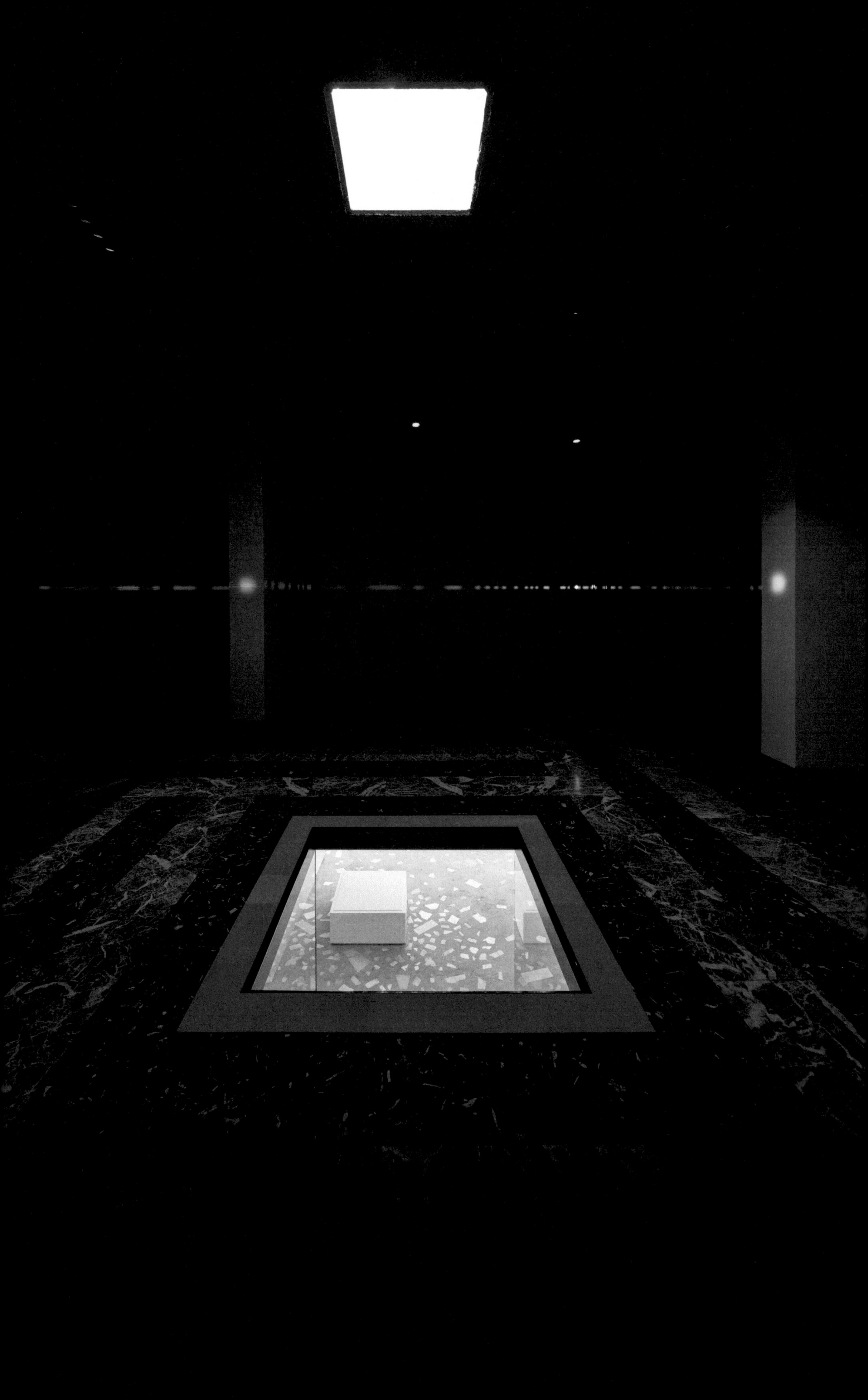

BY WHAT ARE RIVERS FORMED?

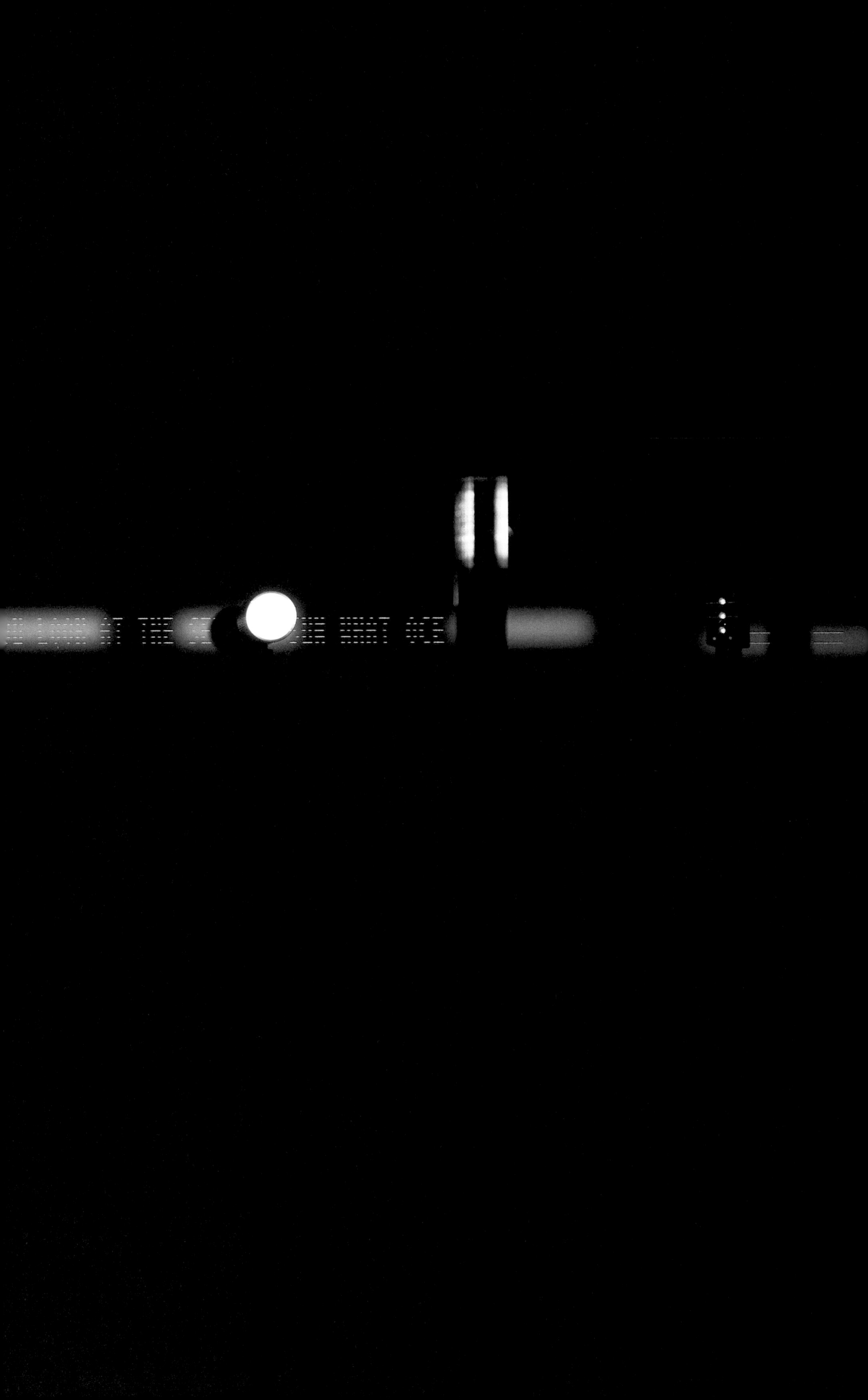

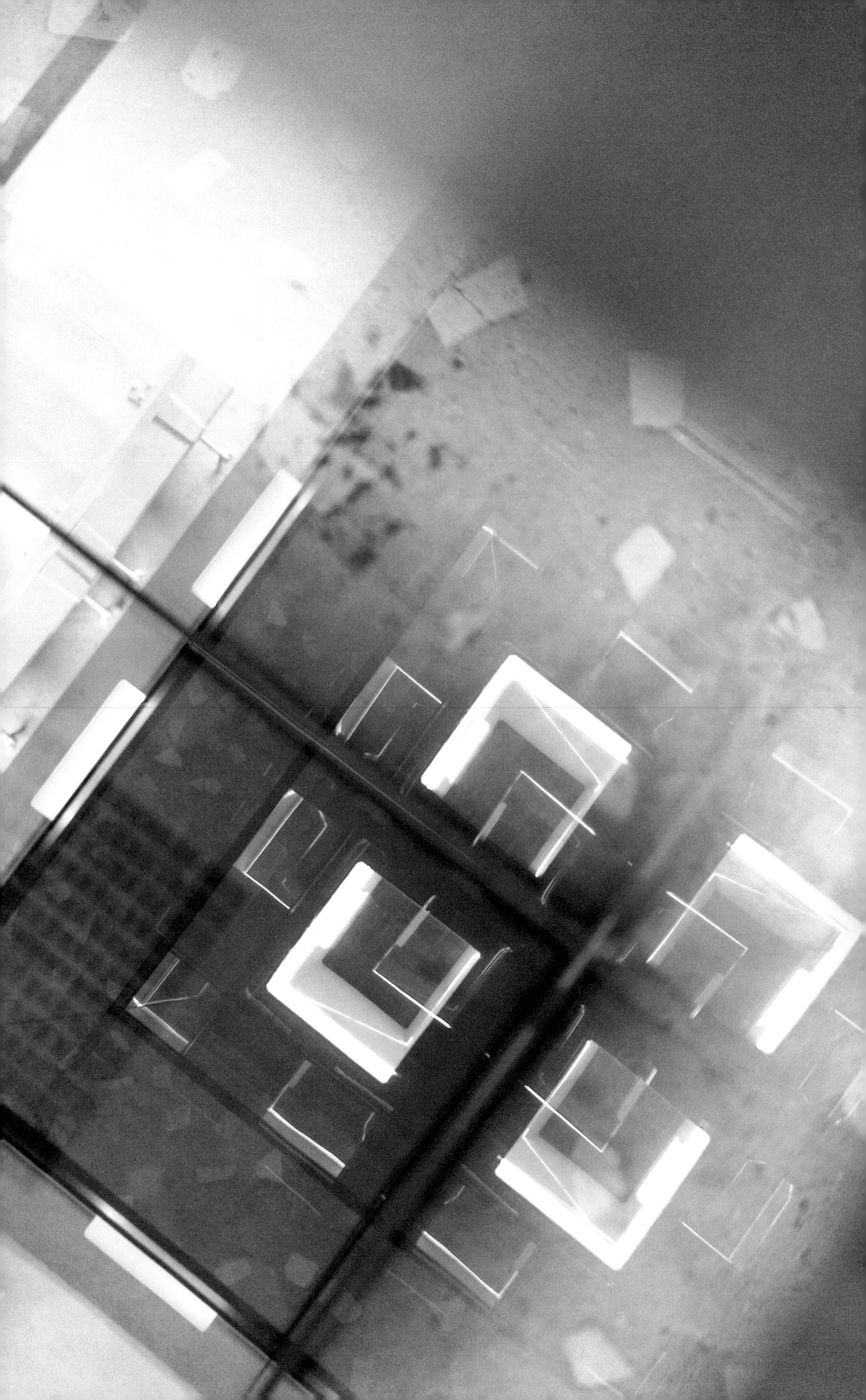

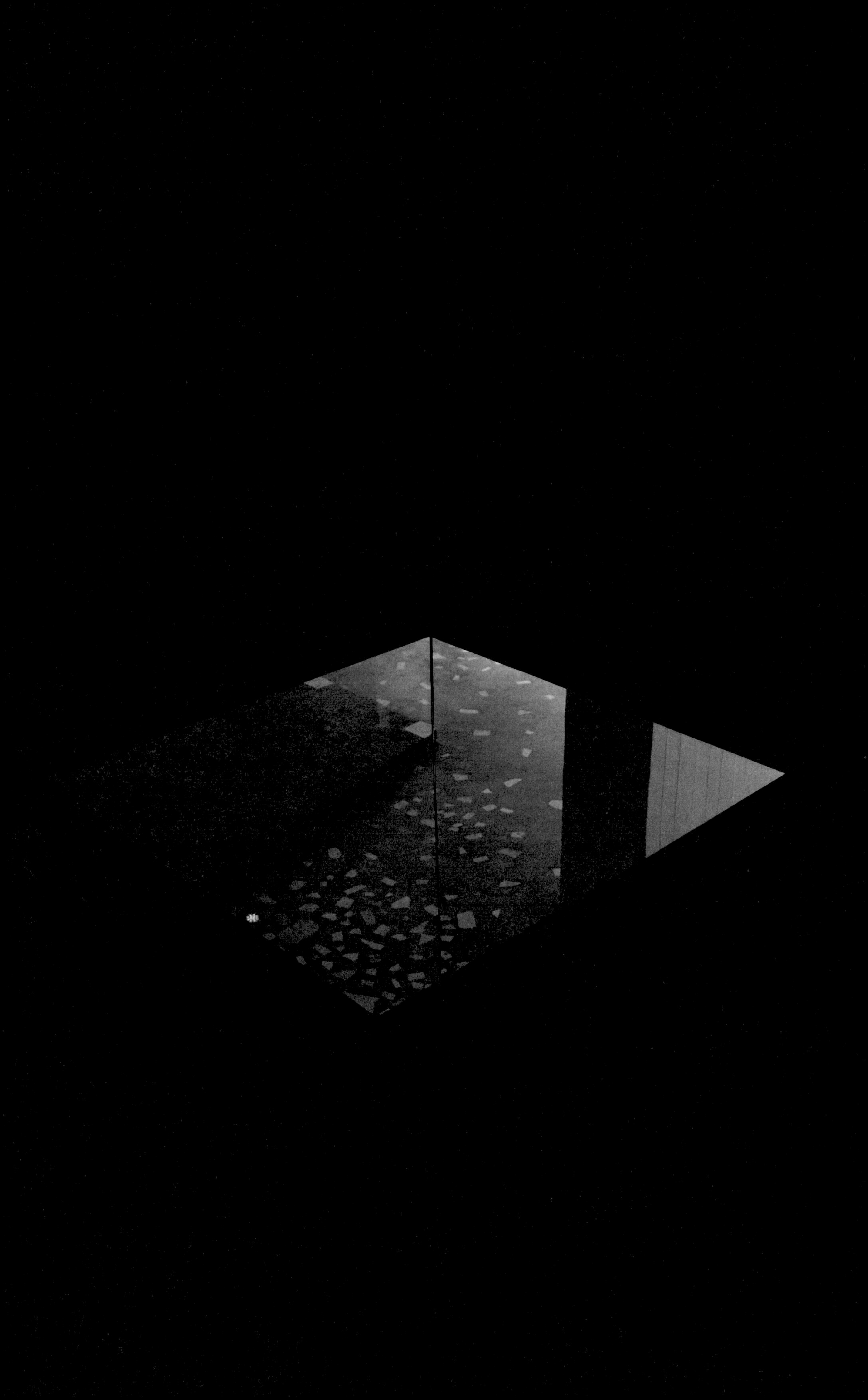

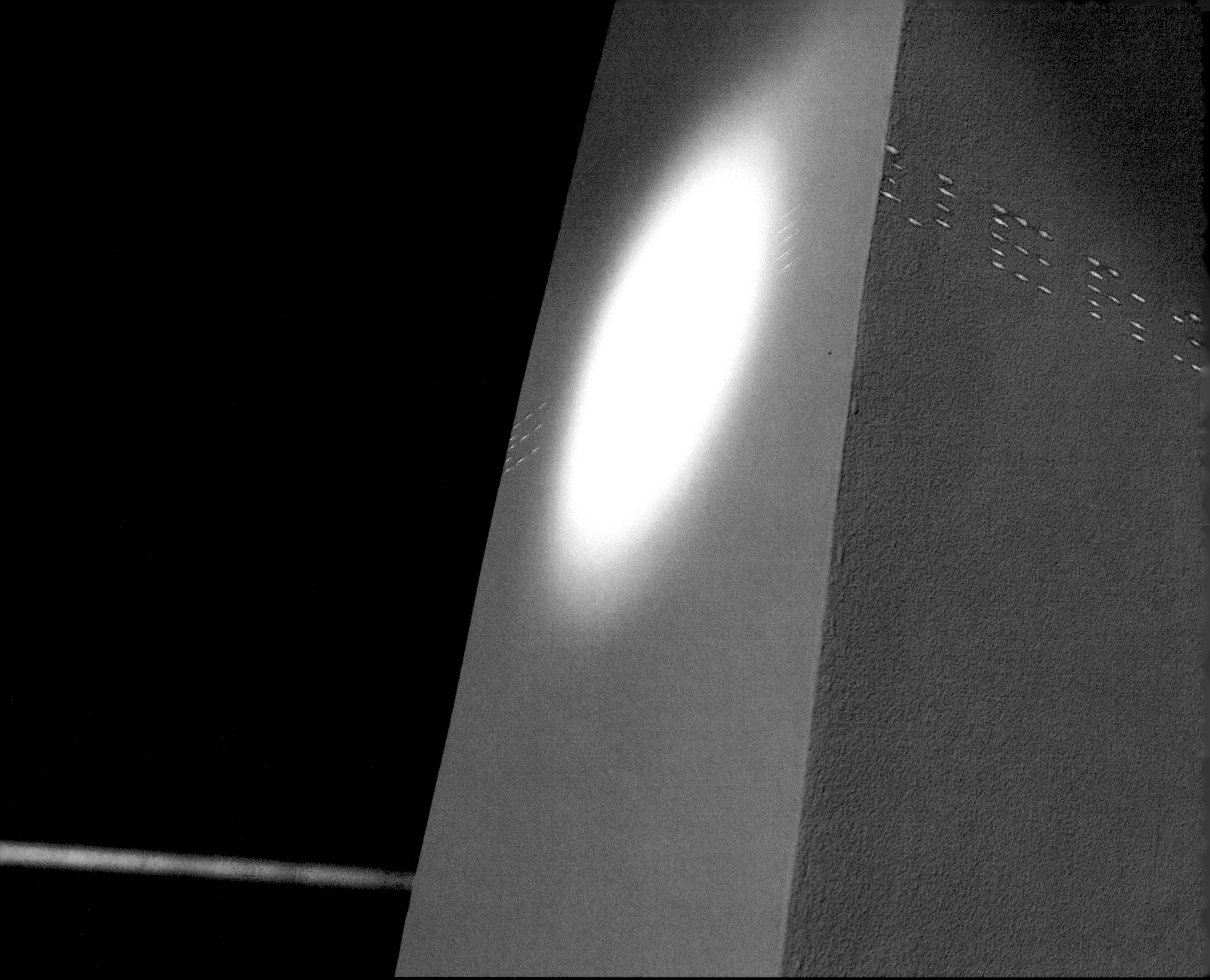

WHEN YOU LOOK AT THE SETTING SUN,

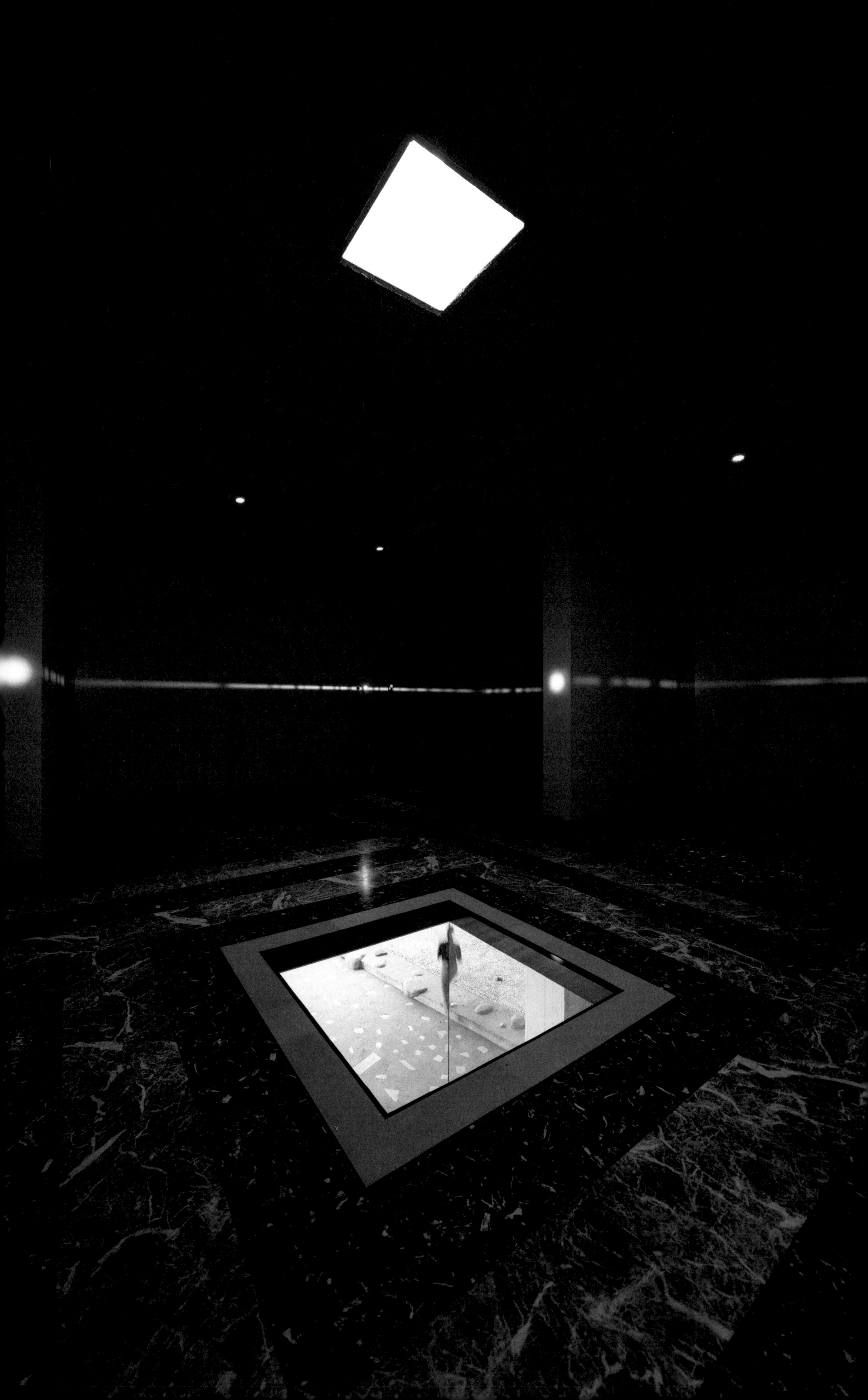

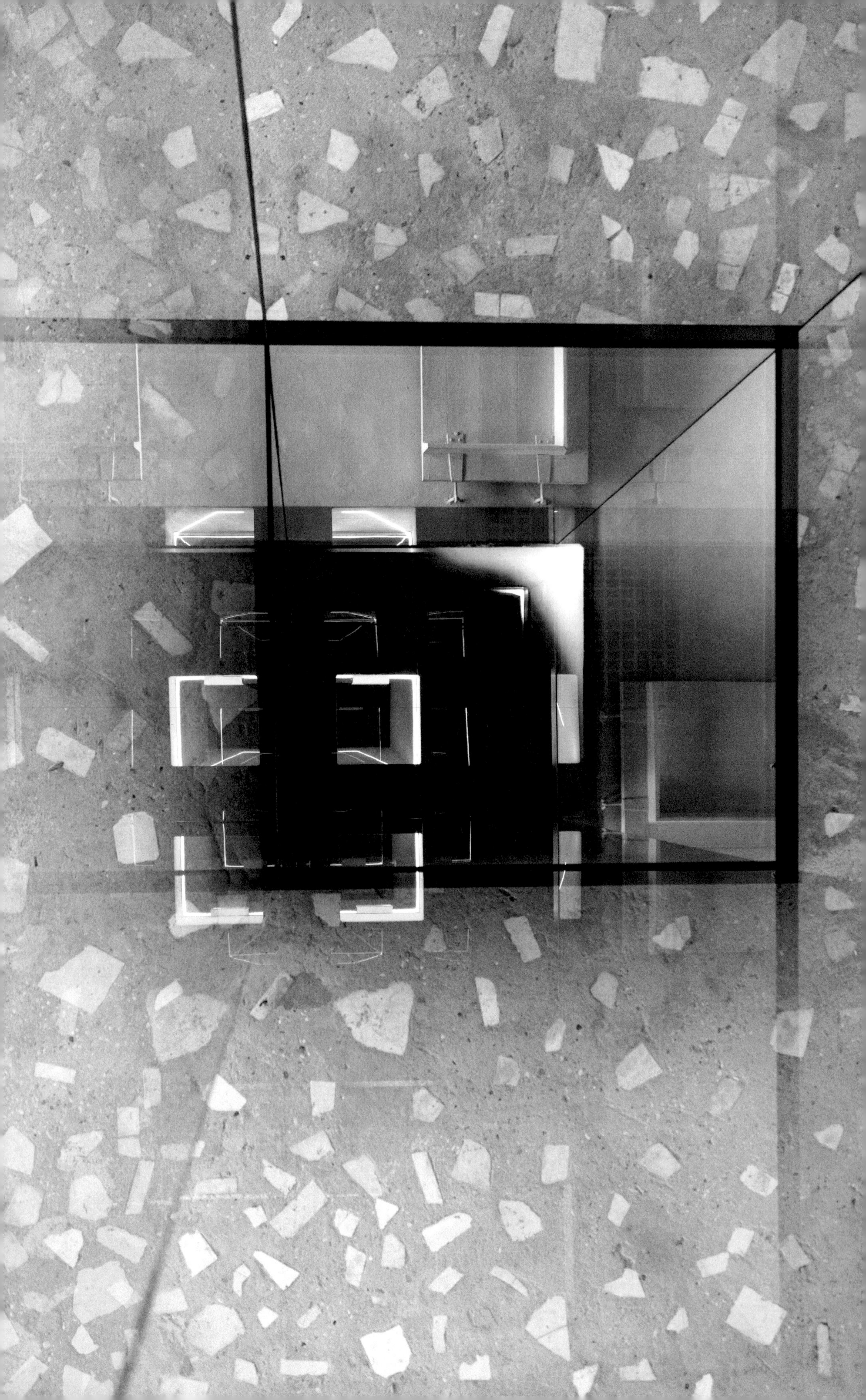

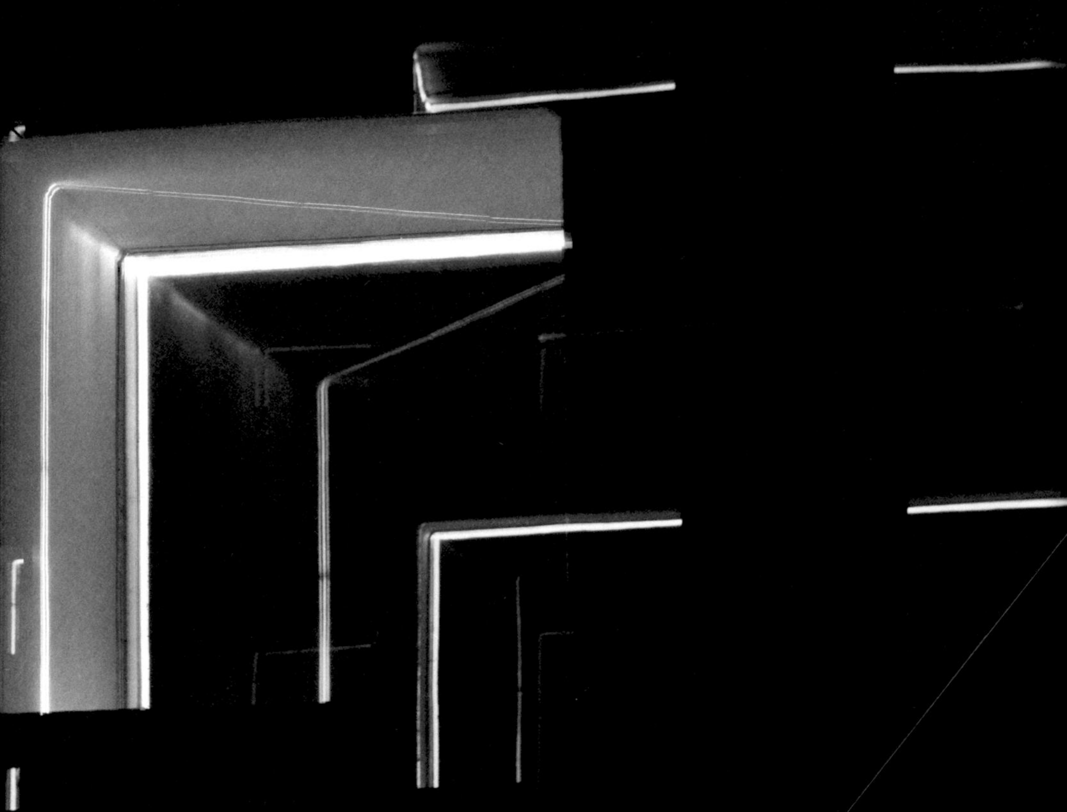

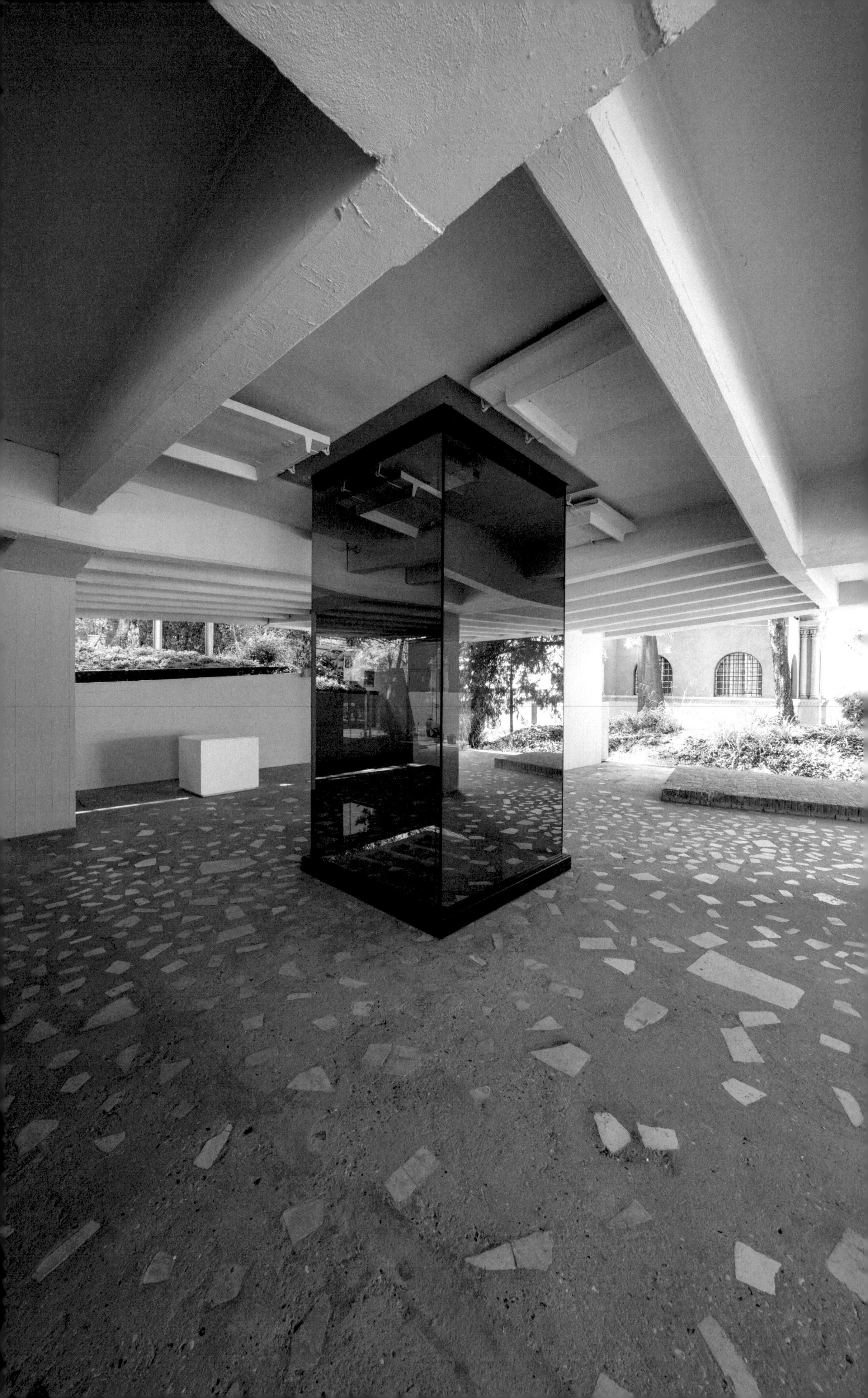

ダムタイプ
2022

ダムタイプ

高谷史郎
坂本龍一
古舘 健
濱 哲史
白木 良
原 摩利彦
泊 博雅
南 琢也
空 里香
高谷桜子

謝辞

声：
デヴィッド・シルヴィアン
竹内真里亜
カヒミ・カリィ
ニキ

フィールド・レコーディング
（2022年5月6日から9月11日まで
Haus der Kunstの「ダムタイプ展」で展示された、
坂本龍一ディレクションによるインスタレーション
《Playback》のために録音された音源）：

Yan Jun｜北京
Crosby Bolani｜ケープタウン
Apichatpong Weerasethakul｜チェンマイ
Kali Malone & Stephen O'Malley｜ラ・トゥール＝ド＝ペ
Mukul Patel｜ロンドン
John Warwicker｜メルボルン
Martin Hernandez｜メキシコシティ
Giuseppe La Spada｜エトナ火山
Damian Lentini｜ミュンヘン
Alec Fellman｜ニューヨーク
Andri Snær Magnason & Kaśka Paluch｜レイキャビク
Jaques Morelenbaum｜リオデジャネイロ
Atom Heart｜サンティアゴ
Cheng Chou｜台北市
Nima Massali｜テヘラン
オノセイゲン｜東京

DUMB TYPE
2022

DUMB TYPE

Shiro Takatani
Ryuichi Sakamoto
Ken Furudate
Satoshi Hama
Ryo Shiraki
Marihiko Hara
Hiromasa Tomari
Takuya Minami
Norika Sora
Yoko Takatani

Acknowledgements

Voices:
David Sylvian
Maria Takeuchi
Kahimi Karie
Niki

Field Recordings
(originally recorded for the installation
Playback directed by Ryuichi Sakamoto
for the Dumb Type Exhibition
at Haus der Kunst Munich in 2022):

Yan Jun | Beijing
Crosby Bolani | Cape Town
Apichatpong Weerasethakul | Chiang Mai
Kali Malone & Stephen O'Malley | La Tour-de-Peilz
Mukul Patel | London
John Warwicker | Melbourne
Martin Hernandez | Mexico City
Giuseppe La Spada | Mount Etna
Damian Lentini | Munich
Alec Fellman | New York
Andri Snær Magnason & Kaśka Paluch | Reykjavik
Jaques Morelenbaum | Rio de Janeiro
Atom Heart | Santiago
Cheng Chou | Taipei
Nima Massali | Tehran
Seigen Ono | Tokyo

日本館展示会場図面
（ジャルディーニ、ヴェネチア、イタリア）

Plan, The Japan Pavilion
Giardini della Biennale, Venezia, Italy

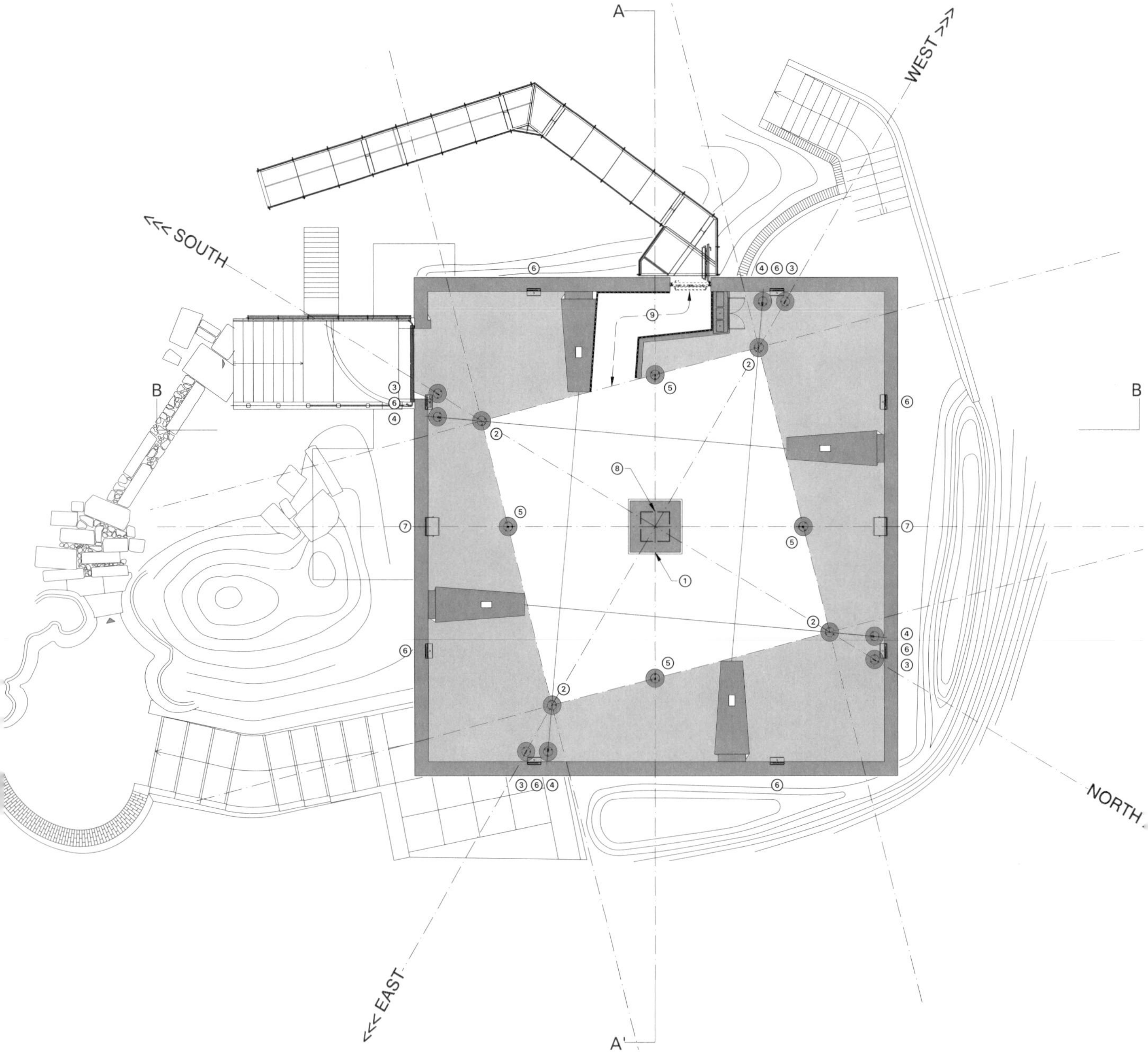

① Half mirror glass box
size: 1638 × 1638 × 3730 mm
passing rate: 25%

② Revolving mirror system
size: ø35 × 2086 mm
× 4 set

③ Laser device
size: 40 × 160 × 2086 mm
× 4 set

④ Collimated beam LED
size: 70 × 70 × 2086 mm
× 4 set

⑤ Revolving parametric speaker
size: 75 × 75 × 1785 mm
× 4 set

⑥ Loudspeaker
Meyer Sound UPM-1P
size: 174 × 457 × 196 mm
× 8 set

⑦ Compact subwoofer
Meyer Sound UMS-1P
size: 578 × 414 × 445 mm

⑧ Eclipse skylight
1000 × 1000 mm, Width 12 mm

⑨ Silent corridor
(Black sound absorbing material)

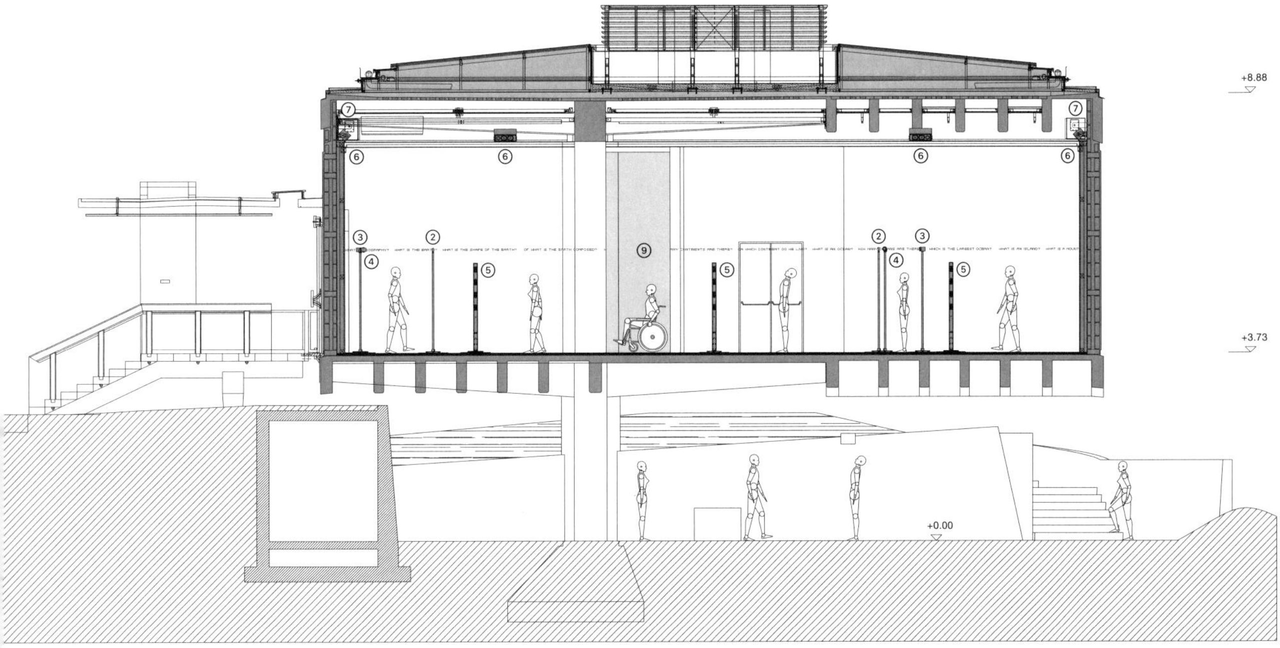

ione A-A′

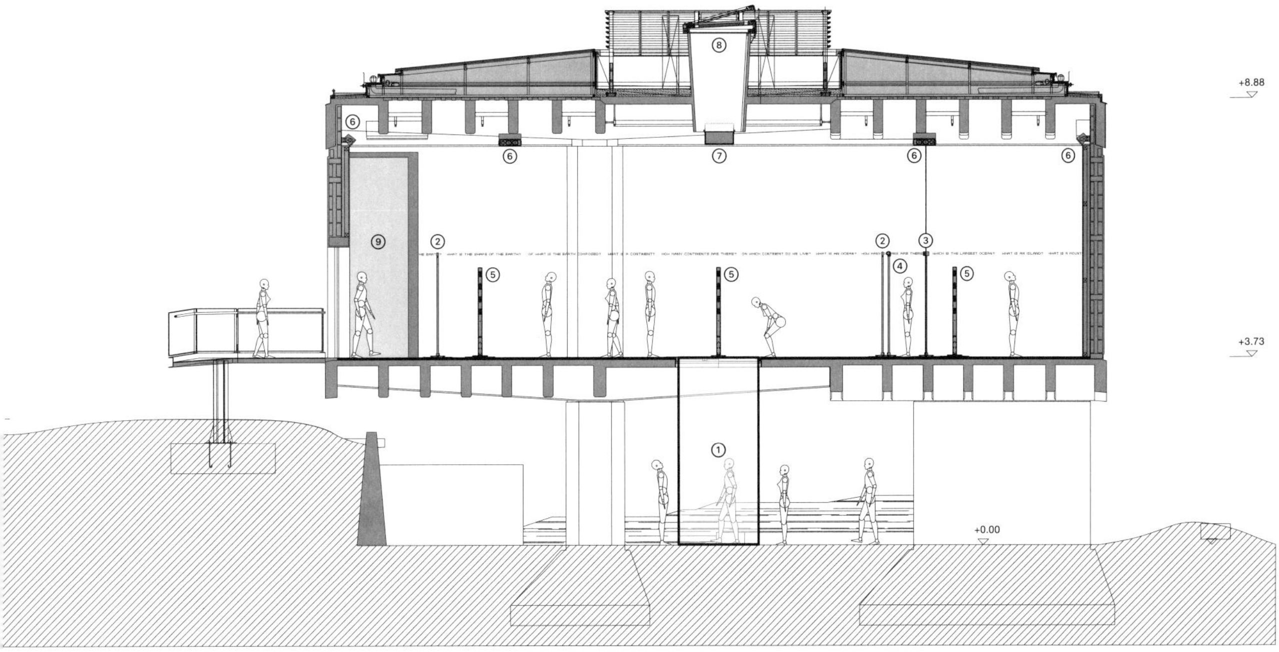

zione B-B′

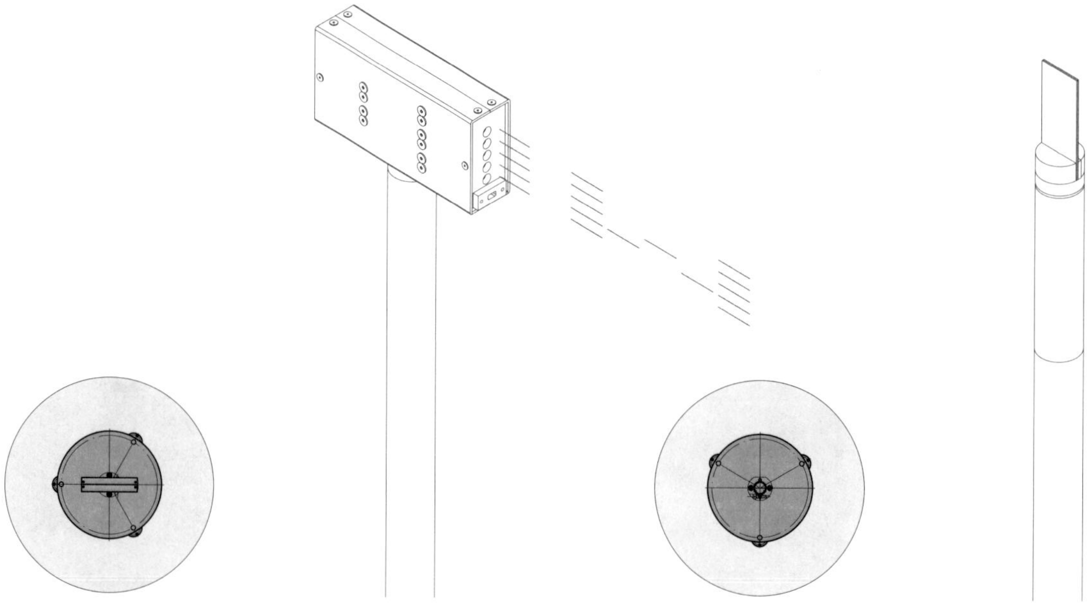

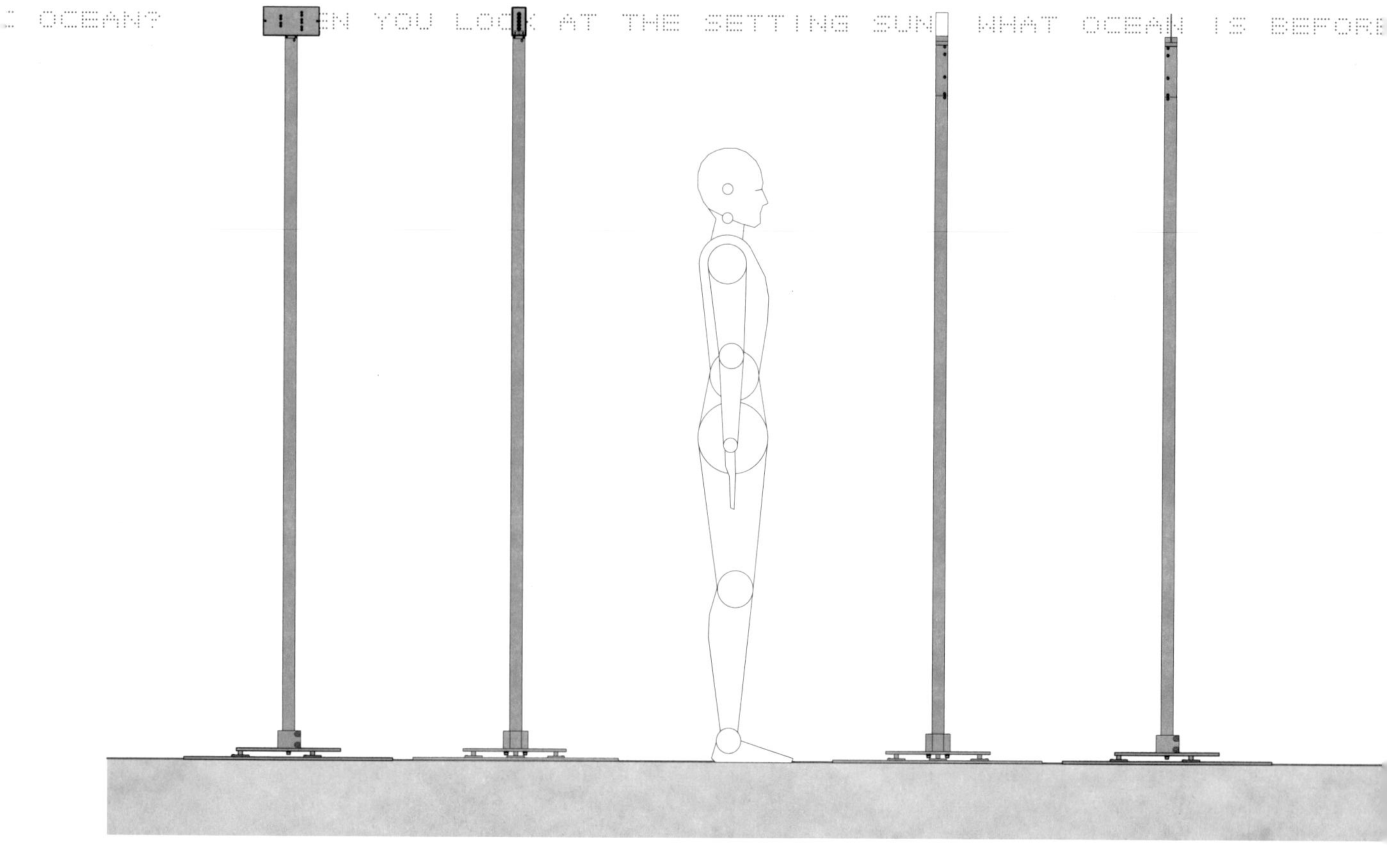

③レーザー装置
5本のレーザー光線を122,800Hzで明滅させて、回転する鏡（②）に反射させることによって文字や信号を壁に投影する装置。

③ Laser device
A device consisting of five laser beams flickering 122,800 times per second, which projects letters and signals onto the walls by means of the revolving mirror (②).

②回転鏡システム
回転する鏡のエンコーダーからの信号（2,048 CPR）と同期して明滅するレーザー光線（③）を鏡に反射させることにより、周囲の壁面に投影して6,144ドットの明暗のグラデーションに展開するシステム。

② Revolving mirror system
A system that reflects the blinking laser beams (③) synchronized with the signals (2,048 CPR) from the encoder of the rotating mirror and projects them onto the surrounding walls to create a gradation of brightness with 6,144 dots of light.

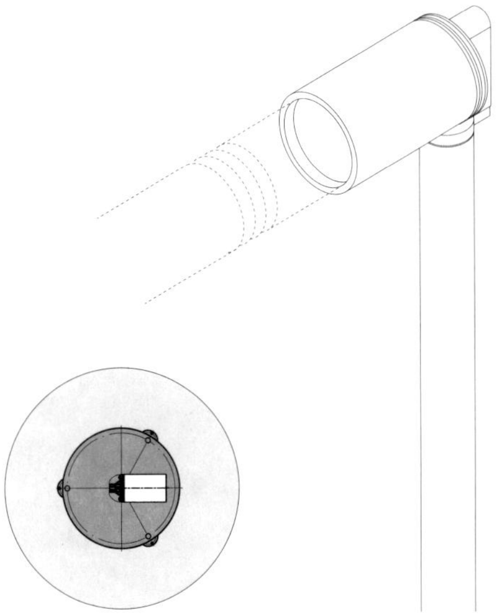

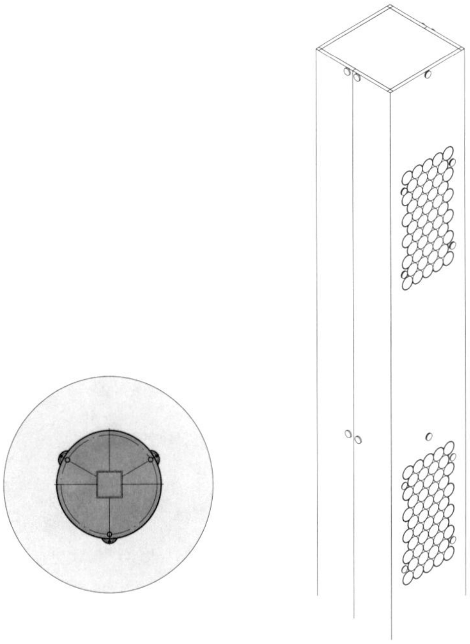

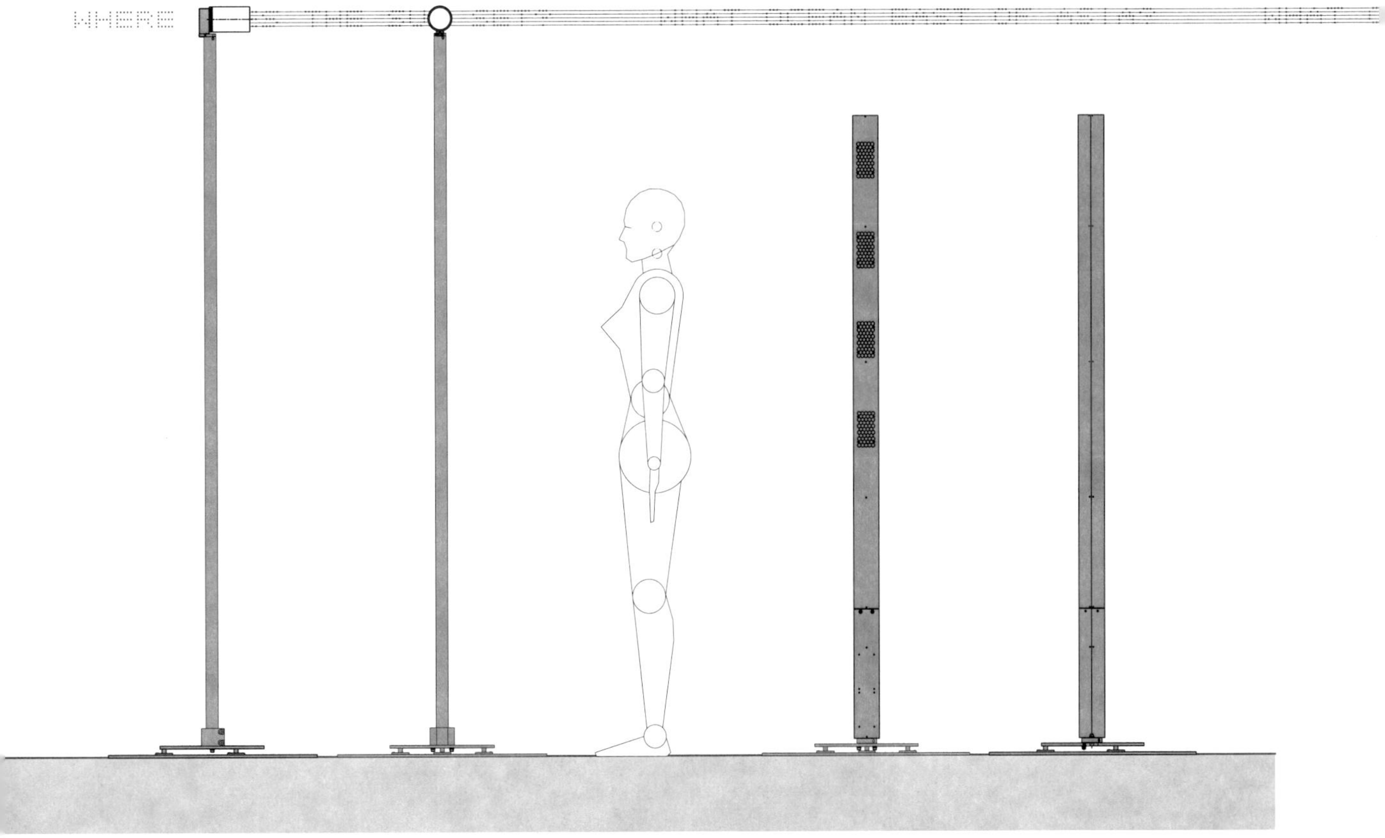

④ 平行光LED
平行光線になるように調整されたLEDライトは1秒間に122,800回明滅し、回転する鏡(②)によって光の帯を壁に投影する。

④ Collimated beam LED
An LED light, adjusted to be a parallel beam, that flickers 122,800 times per second, reflecting off the revolving mirror (②) to create a band of light on the walls.

⑤ 回転式超指向性スピーカー
1 rpm–10 rpm
回転する超指向性スピーカーによって、限定された狭いエリアとその方向だけに音が聞こえるようにコントロール。

⑤ Revolving parametric speaker
1 rpm–10 rpm
A rotating super-directional speaker controls the sound to be heard only in a limited narrow area.

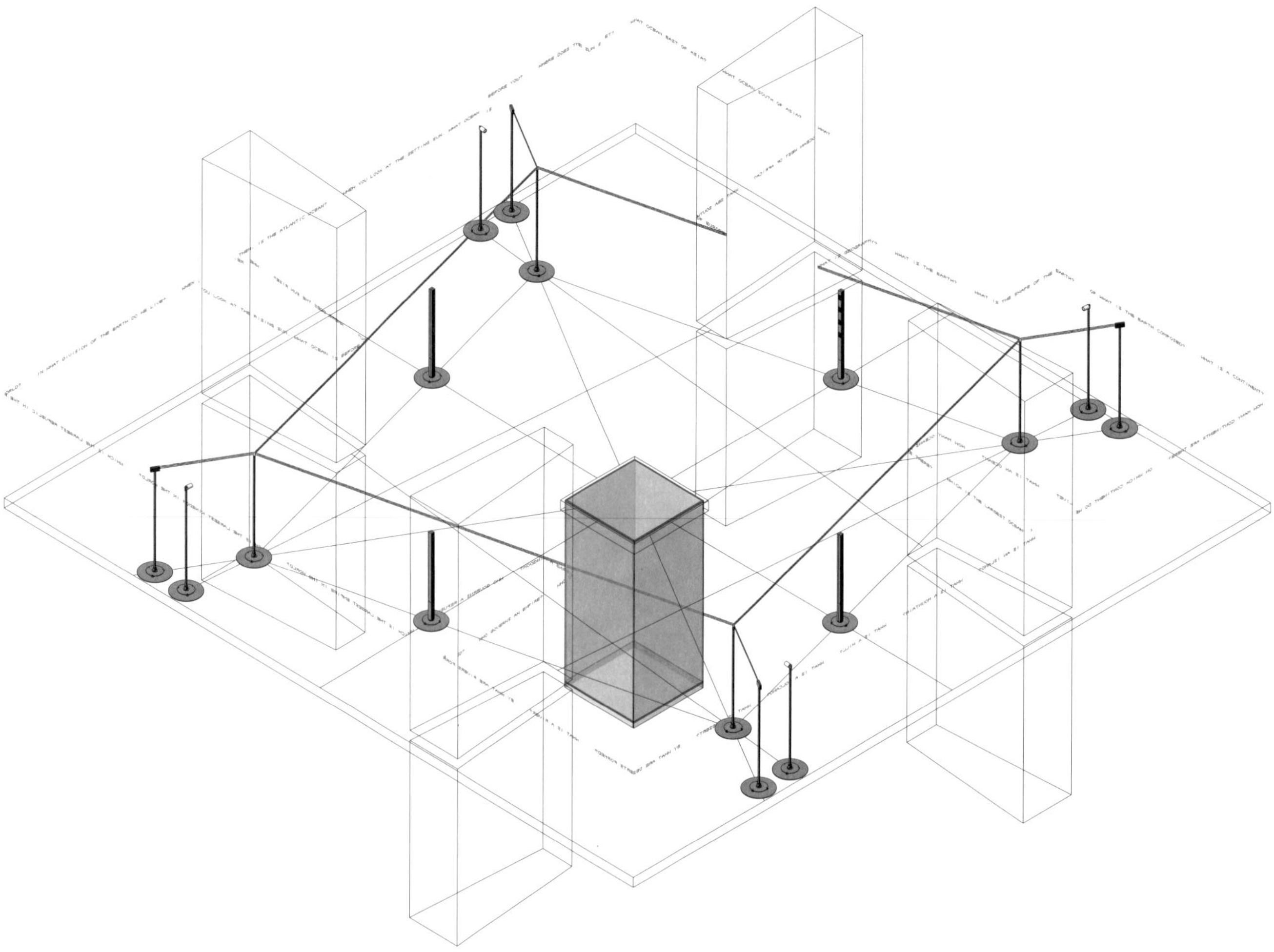
WHAT OCEAN EAST OF ASIA?
WHAT OCEAN SOUTH OF ASIA?
WHAT IS THE EARTH?
WHAT IS THE SHAPE OF THE EARTH?
OF WHAT IS THE EARTH COMPOSED?
WHAT IS A CONTINENT?

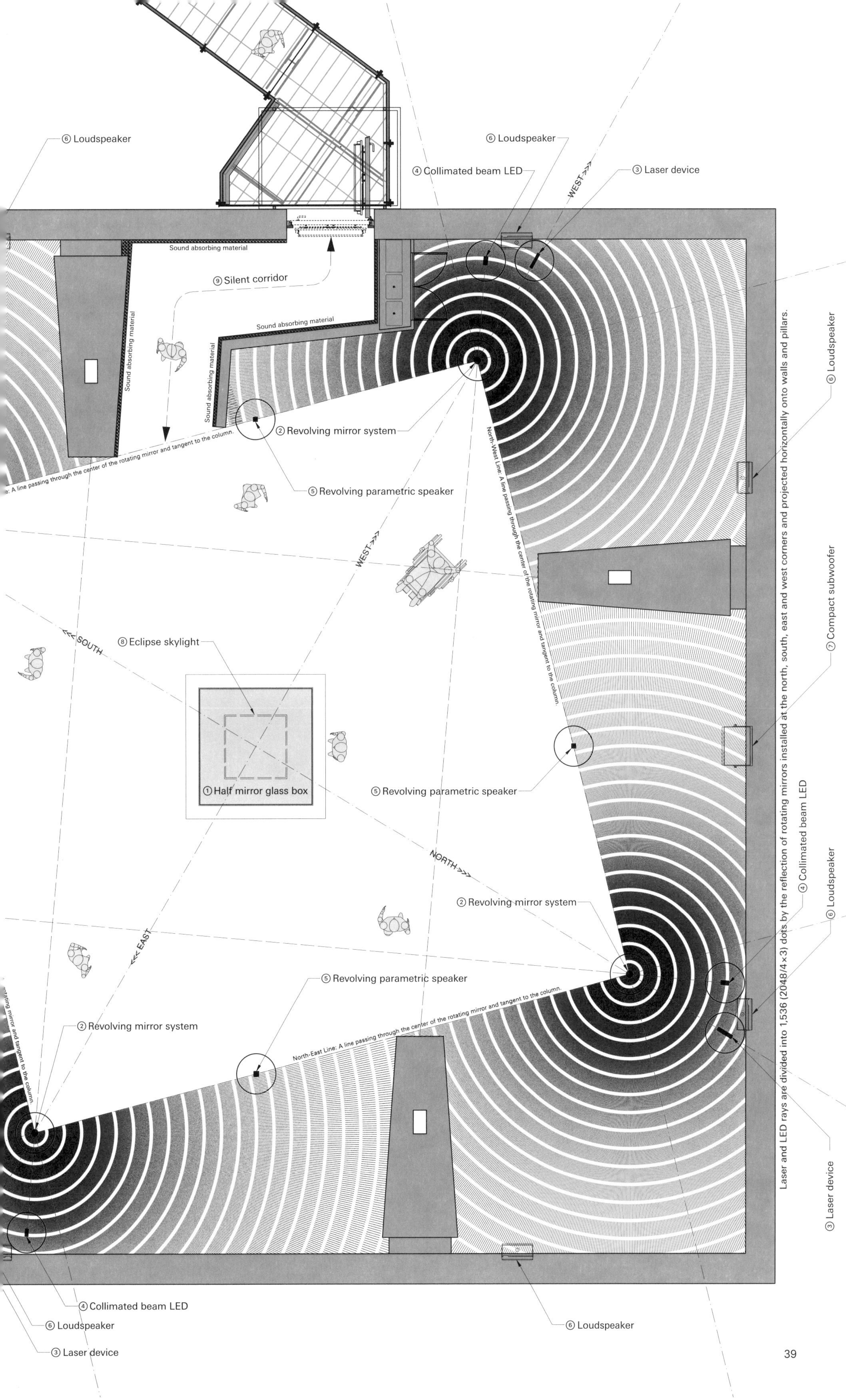

Laser and LED rays are divided into 1,536 (2048/4×3) dots by the reflection of rotating mirrors installed at the north, south, east and west corners and projected horizontally onto walls and pillars.

対話｜坂本龍一＋高谷史郎

──まずは、今回の作品に至る経緯を教えていただけますか?

高谷　ダムタイプは1984年からグループで作品制作してきました。その過程では様々な段階があって、いろいろな制作方法をトライしながら続けてきました。2002年、《Voyage》(パフォーマンス)、《Voyages》(インスタレーション)という作品を発表した後、ダムタイプとしてはしばらく作品制作していなかったんですが、2014年に東京都現代美術館で長谷川祐子さんがキュレーションを担当した展覧会(「東京アートミーティング第5回 新たな系譜学をもとめて—跳躍/痕跡/身体」、2014-15年)にダムタイプへ作品出品の依頼があり、それを機に《MEMORANDUM OR VOYAGE》という作品を制作しました。2018年には、同じく長谷川さんのキュレーションで、ポンピドゥー・センター・メッスでダムタイプの個展(「Dumb Type: Actions + Réflexions」)を開催することになり、《MEMORANDUM OR VOYAGE》に加えて、《Playback》《pH》《LOVE/SEX/DEATH/MONEY/LIFE》の3作品を新しく制作しました。

ダムタイプを始めた頃はコンピューターというものは存在していましたけど、僕たちの技術的にも、当時使うことのできたコンピューターの性能的にも、美術作品としてのクオリティを持つようなものがまだ作れる状態ではありませんでした。当時、コンピューターは技術的にいろいろなことを試しているまだ成長途上段階の時代だったように思います。それと並行して、僕たちは美術やデザインのことを勉強していました。僕たちがコンピューターを作品制作で使えるようになってきたのが90年代中頃ぐらいで、それと同時にビデオプロジェクターも自分たちの手の届く、使える機材になってきたって感覚がありました。技術革新と並行しながら、それに合わせて自分たちのスキル自体も上がってきて、手探りで作ってきたという感じです。

ポンピドゥー・センター・メッスの個展の話をいただいた時、過去の作品を振り返り、現在のプログラム技術を使った新しい解釈で、新しい作品を作ってみようという話になり、《Playback》や《pH》、《LOVE/SEX/DEATH/MONEY/LIFE》を制作しました。それをさらにブラッシュアップしたものを東京都現代美術館では展示することになりました(「ダムタイプ｜アクション+リフレクション」、2019-20年)。そのような時にヴェネチア・ビエンナーレの話があったのですが、ビエンナーレでは「今の延長線上じゃなくて、全く違うものを作りたい」と思ったんです。これまでずっと変化を続けてきたダムタイプが次のフェーズに行けるような作品にしたい。そのためには個人的に長く作品制作をご一緒してきた坂本さんと、ぜひダムタイプで新しい作品を制作したいと思ったんです。

坂本　高谷さんとは長いですよ。一緒に作品を作り出して、20年以上。

高谷　坂本さんは良い意味でダムタイプとは全然違う。僕たちの考え方とは全然違うところからアイデアが出てくる。だから、「本格的にダムタイプに参加してもらえないか」と思ったんです。それはダムタイプも変わらないといけないという意味において。

──ダムタイプの作品制作に参加するというお話は初めてなんですか?

高谷　個人としては山口情報芸術センター[YCAM]やNTTインターコミュニケーション・センター[ICC]ではいくつも一緒に作品制作させてもらっていますが、ダムタイプでコラボレーションするのは初めてです。

坂本　そもそも僕にはダムタイプに入る資格はないですから。年齢も随分と上だし、京都市立芸術大学出身じゃないし(笑)。僕は単なるダムタイプのファンだったんです。だから、ファンでよかったんだけど、「ダムタイプの一員としてなんかやってくれない?」って言われたら……。例えば、あるバンドのファンだとして、「君、バンドに入って、作曲しない？」って言われたら、やばいでしょう。本当に!?　ってなっちゃうよね（笑）。
　声をかけてもらった時、ポンピドゥー・センター・メッスと東京都現代美術館の「ダムタイプ展」で最初から最新まで35年分のアーカイバルな作品を見せるということを徹底的にやられていたので、その続きは確かに難しいだろうなあと思いましたよ。

高谷　そうなんですよ。展覧会はかなりエネルギーを必要とすることなので、それなら違うフェーズに行くエネルギーにしたほうがいいと思いました。でも別にこの先ずっと続けていくことが前提じゃなくて、お互いに影響し合えたらいいなあと。

坂本　変な言い方だけど、ダムタイプは必ず存在しなきゃいけないものでもないからね。

高谷　そうなんです。ずっと存在していなくてもいいんです。

坂本　一人ひとりがバラバラなアーティストでもあるわけで。ダムタイプはそこが他のグループと違うところ。だから出入り自由だし、気が合えばやるし、みたいな感じで、入門試験があるわけでもないし。あったら、僕は落とされるかもしれないけど（笑）。

高谷　いやいや（笑）。

――ダムタイプ主導の作品作りはどのように始まったんですか？

高谷　まずは今までのメンバーで下地作りのミーティングから始めて、ある程度方向性がまとまったら、坂本さんとアイデアの内容を共有しました。すると、坂本さんから「それはどういう意味なんですか？」みたいな返信があって、最初のうちは結構コンセプチュアルなところからやりとりが始まりましたね。ダムタイプはかなり話し合いながら作品作りを進めるので、すごく時間がかかるんです。

――坂本さんが入っても、いつものダムタイプの作り方をされたんですね。

高谷　作品のキーになるテキストを、いかにコンセプトに沿った形で表現できるのか、いつもどおり話し合いを重ねながら進めました。とはいえ、テーマが決まってからは技術的な話がほとんどです。

――坂本さんはそのやり取りをどのように進められたのですか？

坂本　高谷さんから来るアイデアを僕なりに解釈して進めました。最初は光と影の間《あわい》のような話から始まりました。そこからすぐに谷崎潤一郎の『陰翳礼讃』が思い浮かんで。僕の最近作った《TIME》（2021）ともリンクするところがあるテーマだったので考えやすかったです。そして、僕なりにキーワードのようなものを拾っていきました。例えば、ろうそくのジリジリと焼ける音とか、和紙の擦れる音とか。あと以前、僕らが実際に体験したことなんですが、茶室の中にいて、外が急に豪雨になって、室内から雨の音を聞いたことがあって、それが僕らにとっては大きな体験になっていたりして。僕なりに思いつくキーコンセプトを考えて、「間違ってませんよね？」って投げさせてもらいました。

高谷　間違っている、間違っていないという確認もありましたが、「ああ、そうか」って気づくことも多くて、それがすごく面白かったです。自分の中でまだボンヤリした状態のことを坂本さんに投げてしまっているんですが、坂本さんの中で簡潔に整理されて返信が戻ってくるので、すごく頼りにしています（笑）。

坂本　いやいや（笑）。自分が受け取ったことが間違ってないんだということが確認されて、そこからは実際の音を録音してみたり、拾っていったりして、またその音を高谷さんに投げて、「間違ってませんよね？」みたいな音でのやりとりを続けた感じです。

――コンセプトに沿って、音が作られて、それを体験する空間はどのように作られていったのでしょうか？

高谷　とても抽象的なんですが、それぞれの要素を想像しながら空間で構成していくんです。空間と時間というものをコンバートすることは不可能なんですけど、関係している。ここの場所に来ると、このことを思い出すといったような……。時間を空間で覚えていると言えばわかりやすいかな。そんなことを思いながら、空間を構成していった感じです。そこから空間を3Dでモデリングして、坂本さんに投げて、イメージを掴んでもらいながら進めていきました。

――空間で着目すべきポイントはどこでしょうか？

高谷　空間を構成しているアイデアの中には、レーザーやLED、高速回転しているミラーを使用するという技術的な面白さと、坂本さんがお話しされたような実際に自分が体験した寺院の茶室での体験のような「感覚」の面白さ。僕はその両方に興味があって、そこをなんとかマージできないかっていうのが僕にとってはすごく面白い試みになっています。今の分断されている時代にバーチャルな世界の中で人の気配を感じるような感覚と、茶室の中で音によって世界を感じるような感覚。一枚の障子を隔てて外があって、部屋の中でその音や光を感じることで、直接見るよりももっと外を感じることができる。それを新しい技術を使って、うまく表現できているんじゃないかと思っています。

坂本　実際の月を見るのもいいんですけど、障子越しの月明かりのほうが風情があったりしますよね。そこに風が吹いたり、虫が鳴いたり。でもそれは障子越しで見えない。最初に僕たちが一緒に作った作品《LIFE - fluid, invisible, inaudible...》（2007）も、“見えない”とか、“聞こえない”とか、言葉にすると否定的になってしまうんですが、見えないからこそ、想像力で見える。聞こえないからこそ、想像力で聞こえる。一種、日本的な、拡張した想像力の世界だと思うので、そういう意味では、僕たちが作っているものは一貫していると思います。僕はそういうコンセプトが好き。見せることよりも見せないことのほうが大事なんじゃないかという引き算。日本らしい表現で、ヴェネチア・ビエンナーレの日本館でやる意味があると思います。

高谷　坂本さんと一緒に作らせていただいた《TIME》から、僕はかなり影響を受けています。その作品作りのために、坂本さんから勧めてもらった本を読んだり、お話を聴いたりして。そういう意味では全て連続しているんです。《LIFE - fluid, invisible, inaudible...》があって、《TIME》があって、その間に《water state 1》（2013）という自然の変化を取り入れた作品を作っていて、どんどんつながって、今に至っている。今回はダムタイプとしての作品制作ですけど、僕の中ではずっとつながってきている。それがちょっと面白く変化していけばいいなと思っています。

坂本　高谷さんは地続きであるとおっしゃってくれていますが、僕からすると、ダムタイプのメンバーとして作品を作るということがあるとないとでは大きく違ったかもしれない。だから、音を送った時も、「ダムタイプっぽくないと思ったら、カットしてください」「なんでも言ってください」と伝えていました。新人メンバーなんで（笑）。

高谷　「ダムタイプっぽい」というものは、今このメンバーで作っていくものだと思っています。そもそもあるようでないようなものですし、メンバーによっても変わっていきますし。

ただ、送ってもらった音を聴いた時、想像していたものと違ったんですよね。インスタレーションの音というよりは、映画のサウンドトラックのような壮大なひとつのまとまった音楽でした。僕の中ですぐに映像が浮かんできた。すごくいいトラックだと思ったんですけども、これをインスタレーションの作品にすると考えたら、そんな頭でこの音楽を聴いていては駄目だなと思ったんです。だから、音楽にはアダプトしつつ、インスタレーション作品としてどう捉えていこうかと考えました。
　今回使用している自作の回転式超指向性スピーカーは聴く場所によって音が異なるので、鑑賞者ひとりずつ違う音の体験ができる。例えば、このサウンドトラックの中でこの音だけを聴けて、この音は聴けないとなれば、普通のスピーカーで聴いているものとは違う密度を作り出せる。そうやって空間で切り分けていけば、インスタレーションとしての音響空間作品が成立するんじゃないかと思って。坂本さんはそれを想像して作曲されていたんだと思うんですけど、僕は形にしながら「坂本さん、すげえ」って改めて思っていました（笑）。

坂本　別にサウンドトラック的なものを作ろうと思ったわけではないんですよ。大本のコンセプトに沿って、この音が合うかな？　と作っていって、それが音的に馴染むように試行錯誤しながら並び替えただけ。それが絶対というわけではない。音楽の場合、ドミソの次にヘンテコな音がきたら“間違い”になるけど、インスタレーションの音というのは、それが“間違い”にはならない。その時の自分が聴いて、「この次はこの音に変わったほうがいいよね」って、感覚で置いていって、他のものとも取り替えても構わないというぐらいのスタンスで自由に決定して、音を置いていっています。

高谷　自由なんだけど、空間で切り分けるだけで、時間軸として、音の密度を変えることができるのが面白いんです。通常のスピーカーで全体の音を聴くと情報がずっと続いているようだけど、超指向性スピーカーを使って空間で聴き分けていくと、情報が切り分けられて面白い体験になる。今まで、インスタレーションでは何かの法則で音が変化していくという考え方でしたけど、今回は全体のひとつながりの時間もありつつ、それぞれの空間のポジションで各々が違う体験ができるという作り方になっています。

坂本　音楽の時間というリニアで二次元のものを三次元で配置するというのは面白いですよね。聴こえ方も全然違う。

高谷　坂本さんがICCの《IS YOUR TIME》（2017）で、複数の演奏者に展示室内をランダムに歩いてもらうというパフォーマンスイベントをしたじゃないですか。今回は、演奏者（スピーカー）は動かないけれど、音が室内を移動していくという体験ですよね。

坂本　ひとつの流れのある音楽ではあるんだけど、その音の発生源がどんどん動いていく。だから聴く人がどこにいるかで聴こえ方が変わってしまう。スピーカーを回転させることで、その体験が作り出されている。

高谷　どんなインスタレーションでもコンサートでも、厳密に言うと体験する場所でそれぞれ違う音を聴いているんです。でも、今の基本となっているPAシステムはできるだけ均等な音をサービスするシステム。この作品ではそうじゃなくて、もっと局所的にある音を届けるようなシステムにした感じです。鑑賞者それぞれが違う音の体験をして、一人ひとりが「互いのコミュニケーション」ということを考えたり、想像してもらえたら、そういう体験になればと思います。

（2022年2月、京都にて　聞き手：伊藤総研）

— Can you tell us how this work came about?

Takatani: Dumb Type has been creating artworks as a group since 1984. During the process, we went through various phases, experimenting with different production methods. After presenting the performance *Voyage* and the installation *Voyages* in 2002, Dumb Type, as a group, went on a bit of a hiatus. But in 2014, Yuko Hasegawa was curating an exhibition for the Museum of Contemporary Art Tokyo and she asked us to participate, which led to the creation of *MEMORANDUM OR VOYAGE*. Then, in 2018, she curated a solo exhibition of Dumb Type for the Centre Pompidou-Metz, where we produced new versions of three pieces: *Playback, pH,* and *LOVE/SEX/DEATH/MONEY/LIFE,* in addition to *MEMORANDUM OR VOYAGE.*

When we started Dumb Type, computers already existed, but we were not skilled enough to use them to create anything worth presenting as artwork. Also, the computers we were able to use at the time did not have enough performance to produce art works. Back then, I think computers were still in a stage of growth and technical experimentation. At the same time, we were learning about art and design. It was around the mid-90s when we began to use computers in our productions. Simultaneously, we felt video projectors were becoming more accessible to us. Alongside technological innovation, our skills improved, and we continued to create works through trial and error.

For our solo exhibition *DUMB TYPE: Actions + Reflections* at the Centre Pompidou-Metz, we reflected on our past works and had the idea of reinterpreting some of them with contemporary programming technology to create new works. That's what we did with *Playback*, *pH*, and *LOVE/SEX/DEATH/MONEY/LIFE.* Later, we polished them further to exhibit at the Museum of Contemporary Art Tokyo. It was then that we were approached about the Venice Biennale. Thinking about Venice, we wanted to create something completely different, as opposed to just an extension of what we'd already done. Dumb Type has always been evolving, and we wanted to create a work that would take us to the next phase. Based on that thought, I had the idea of making something new with Ryuichi Sakamoto, with whom I have personally worked for a long time.

Sakamoto: Shiro Takatani and I have been working together for a long time. We've been creating works together for more than 20 years now.

Takatani: Ryuichi is totally different in a good way. His ideas come from a completely different place than ours. So, we thought, "Why don't we formally ask Ryuichi to join Dumb Type?" We wanted to work with him, especially because we were thinking Dumb Type needs to change.

— Was this the first time you asked him to collaborate under the Dumb Type name?

Takatani: We have collaborated on a number of works at YCAM and ICC, but this was the first time as Dumb Type.

Sakamoto: First off, I don't feel like I meet the Dumb Type qualifications. I didn't graduate from the Kyoto City University of Arts, and I'm a lot older. I was just a fan of theirs, and I was happy to stay that way, but they asked me, "Would you work with us as a member of Dumb Type?" It's as if a band you liked asked you to join and make music with them. You'd be like, "Are you serious?"

When they approached me, they had just showcased 35 years of Dumb Type's archival works—comprehensively from the earliest pieces to the most recent—for the Centre Pompidou-Metz and the Museum of Contemporary Art Tokyo, so I recognized the difficulty of following that up.

Takatani: That's right. Exhibitions require a lot of energy, so I thought it would be better to use it to move towards a different phase. However, continuing to work together in the future was not a prerequisite. I just thought it would be good if we could influence each other.

Sakamoto: This may sound weird, but Dumb Type doesn't necessarily have to keep going.

Takatani: Exactly. It doesn't have to exist forever.

Sakamoto: Every member of Dumb Type is an artist in their own right. That's what sets Dumb Type apart from other groups. So, everyone is free to come and go, and join in when it feels right. There is no entrance exam. If there were, I might be rejected!

Takatani: No, no, ...

—— So how did Dumb Type initiate the process of creation?

Takatani: We started with the usual members of Dumb Type to set the groundwork. Once we agreed on a certain direction, we shared our ideas with Ryuichi. Then, Ryuichi would ask, "What do you mean by that?" That's how our conversation began. The exchange started from a rather conceptual place. Dumb Type always takes time to make work because we have a lot of discussions during the process.

—— So even with Mr. Sakamoto's participation, you followed the usual Dumb Type method of creation.

Takatani: Yes, it felt like we proceeded as usual, with many discussions. We considered how the key text could express the concept. However, once we had decided on the theme, most of our conversations were technical.

—— Mr. Sakamoto, what did you think about these discussions?

Sakamoto: I interpreted the ideas that came from Shiro in my own way and proceeded from there. At first, we started talking about the space between light and shadow. I immediately thought of Jun'ichirō Tanizaki's *In Praise of Shadows*. It came to me quickly because it linked up with my recent work, *TIME*. Then, in my own way, I picked up key ideas as I went along. For example, the sound of a candle burning or sheets of *washi paper* rubbing together. Also, this is from a shared experience, but one time, we were in a tea ceremony room when it suddenly started pouring. We sat there, listening to the sound of the rain from inside the room, which was a significant experience for us. I thought of a few key concepts and asked whether I was headed in the right direction.

Takatani: Of course, we checked in to make sure we were on the right track, but there were many times when these conversations became discoveries. That was very interesting for me. I would throw something super vague at Ryuichi, to which he would reply in a concise and organized manner. Reading his responses reassured me. I rely on him a lot!

Sakamoto: Not that much! Anyway, once I confirmed that my interpretation was on point, from there, I would try to record or find sounds, then throw them over to Shiro, asking him, "Is this right?" That's how we exchanged our sound ideas.

—— So you had the concept and created the sounds.
How did you create the space in which they are experienced?

Takatani: It was very abstract, but I would imagine every element and compose them in space. It is impossible to convert space or time, but they're related. For example, a specific place may make you recall a certain memory. It might be easier to understand if I say that we remember time through space. I structured the space with this in mind. From there, I modeled the space in 3D, passed it to Ryuichi, and asked him to continue his process while imagining the space.

— What are some of the important elements that make up the space?

Takatani: Some of the ideas are technically interesting, such as the use of lasers, LEDs, and spinning mirrors. But, it is also interesting in relation to the experience in the tea room that Ryuichi shared. I am intrigued by both aspects, and it was an experiment for me to see if I could merge the two. Using new technology, I wanted to create a feeling of the presence of others within a virtual world in our divided era, along with the sensation of the world outside of the tea room that you can sense through sound. Ryuichi said that we can experience the outer world better when we are separated from it by a single sheet of paper, feeling the sound and light inside of the room, rather than experiencing what's out there directly. I think we were able to express this well.

Sakamoto: Looking at the actual moon is nice, but moonlight through a paper screen has a distinct elegance. The wind blows and the insects chirp, but you can't see them through the paper. That was the theme of the first work we made together: *LIFE - fluid, invisible, inaudible....* Words like "invisible" or "inaudible" have a negative connotation, but it is because they are invisible or inaudible that you can see or hear more clearly through your imagination. It is a kind of Japanese world of extended imagination. In that sense, the theme in our work is consistent. I'm pretty interested in this concept. Subtraction is more important—to obscure rather than show. It is a particularly Japanese approach, and I think it is meaningful to have it in the Japanese Pavilion at the Venice Biennale.

Takatani: I'm greatly influenced by the experience of creating *TIME* with Ryuichi. While making it, I read several books that he recommended and listened to his ideas. In that way, everything we've made is continuous. There was *LIFE - fluid, invisible, inaudible...,* then *TIME*, and in between, we created *water state 1*, a work incorporating natural changes. All of these connect and lead to what we're doing now. This time, we're making work as Dumb Type, but they're all related in my mind. I hope new exciting things are to come.

Sakamoto: Shiro is kind to say they're all connected, but from my point of view, it feels different to make something as a member of Dumb Type. So, when I initially sent him the sounds, I told him "If it doesn't feel like Dumb Type, just cut it." Since I'm a new member, I made sure to tell them to not hold anything back.

Takatani: I think "Dumb Type-ness" is defined by whatever comes out of the members at the time. It may or may not exist in the first place, and it changes depending on the members. But, I will say that when I heard the sounds you sent, they were not what I had imagined. Rather than a sound for an installation, it felt like an epic piece of cohesive music, like the soundtrack to a movie. Images came to me immediately. I thought it was a great track, but I also thought I had to change my mindset when thinking of it as part of the installation. So, I considered how to adapt to the music and capture it as an installation piece.

With our custom rotating super-directional speakers, you can hear different sounds depending on where you listen from, so each person will have a unique sonic experience. For example, if you can distill a specific sound from the others within the soundtrack, you can create a different density than what you would get out of a typical speaker. By breaking up the space in this way, we can create a sonic spatial artwork that functions as an installation piece. I think Ryuichi composed the music while imagining this, but when I was actually organizing the space, I was constantly astounded by what he did.

Sakamoto: I didn't really set out to create a soundtrack. I found sounds that seemed to be in line with the concept and rearranged everything so that it would blend sonically. Nothing was set in stone. When listening to music, if you get a sequence of notes "C," "E," "G," and a strange sound comes after, you would interpret it as an error. But, within an installation, it isn't necessarily a mistake. I would listen to the music and think, "This one should come next" and orchestrate the sounds based on my sensibility. I made sure I was free to change the sounds.

Takatani: It's fascinating because there's a lot of freedom to change the density of sound within time by slicing up the space. When you listen to sound through standard speakers, the information flows continuously. In our installation, sound is separated with super-directional speakers, making for a more exciting experience. In our past installations, we based the sound changes on a specific pattern, but in this work, you have the overall time of the piece itself. The result is different depending on how you experience it.

Sakamoto: It's interesting to make something that is linear and two-dimensional like musical time and place it in three-dimensional space. The way you hear it is completely different.

Takatani: During our exhibition *IS YOUR TIME* at ICC, you did a performance event in which you had multiple performers randomly walk around the exhibition space. This time, the performers (speakers) stay in one place, but the sounds move around in the space.

Sakamoto: The music is a single stream, but the source of the sounds continuously moves. Therefore, how the sound is heard depends on the listener's position. Rotating the speakers is what produces this experience.

Takatani: Strictly speaking, any installation or concert will have a different sound depending on where you experience it. The PA systems most often used today, however, try to balance the sound as much as possible. In this piece, the system is designed to deliver a specific sound locally. I hope that everyone who experiences this work will have a unique sonic experience, and that they will each think about how to communicate with each other—that's what I want people to take away.

February 2022 in Kyoto

Interview: Soken Ito
Translation: Neo Sora, Hibiki Mizuno

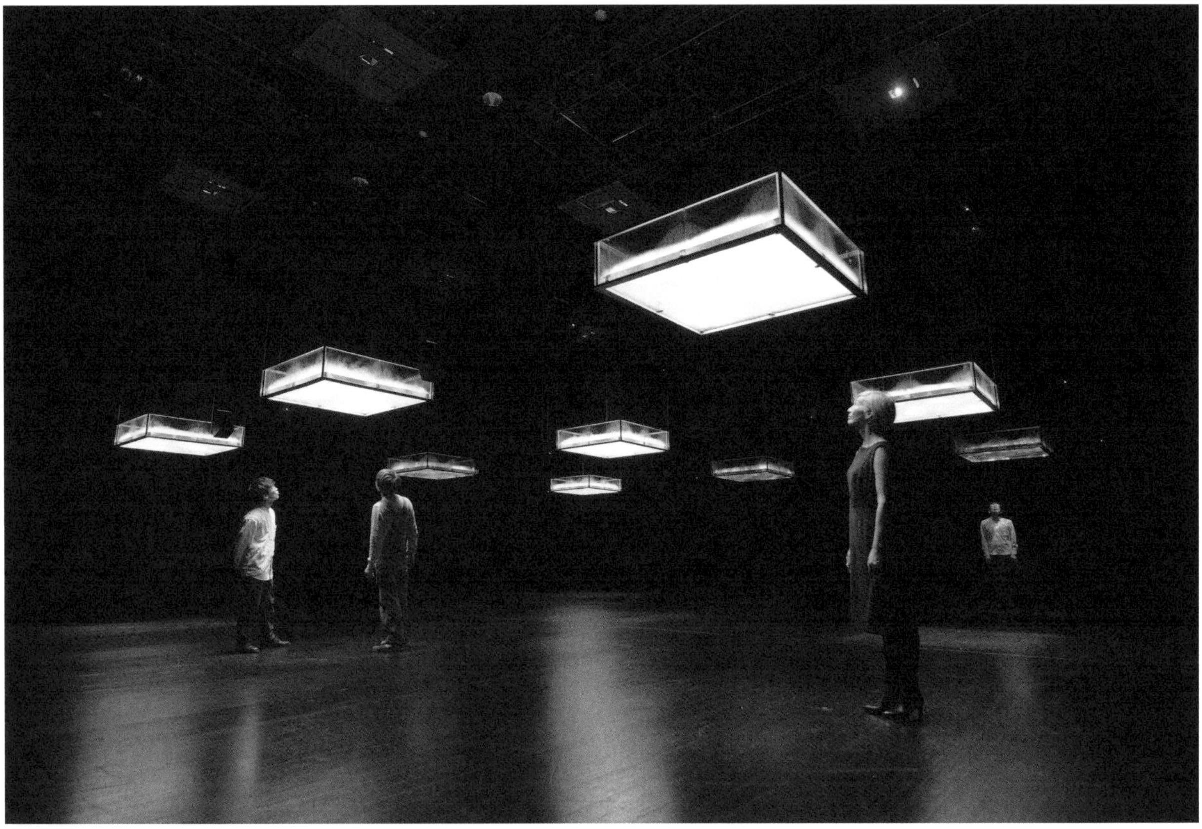

LIFE - fluid, invisible, inaudible... | 2007
坂本龍一 + 高谷史郎
山口情報芸術センター［YCAM］委嘱作品
撮影：山中慎太郎（Qsyum!）
写真提供：山口情報芸術センター［YCAM］

LIFE - fluid, invisible, inaudible... | 2007
Ryuichi Sakamoto + Shiro Takatani
Commissioned by Yamaguchi Center for Arts and Media [YCAM]
Photo: Shintaro Yamanaka (Qsyum!)
Courtesy of Yamaguchi Center for Arts and Media [YCAM]

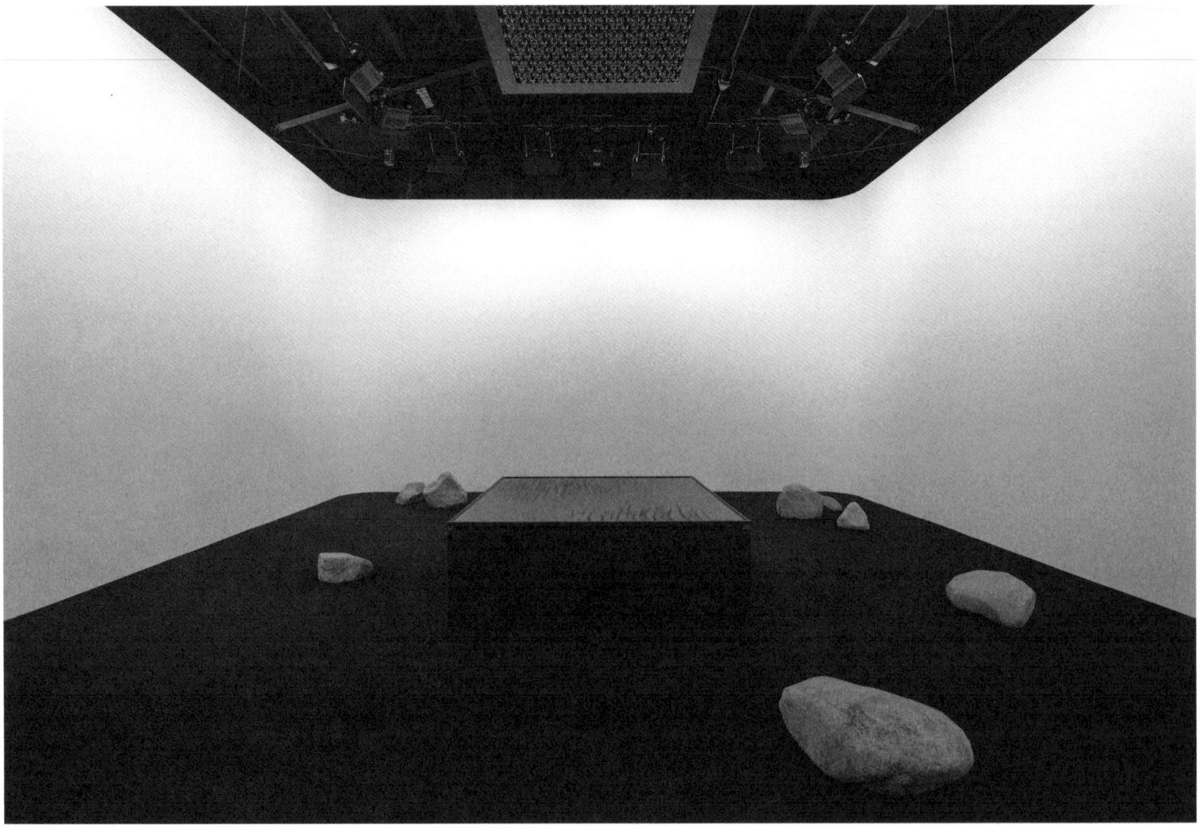

water state 1 | 2013
坂本龍一 + 高谷史郎
山口情報芸術センター［YCAM］委嘱作品
撮影：山中慎太郎（Qsyum!）
写真提供：山口情報芸術センター［YCAM］

water state 1 | 2013
Ryuichi Sakamoto + Shiro Takatani
Commissioned by Yamaguchi Center for Arts and Media [YCAM]
Photo: Shintaro Yamanaka (Qsyum!)
Courtesy of Yamaguchi Center for Arts and Media [YCAM]

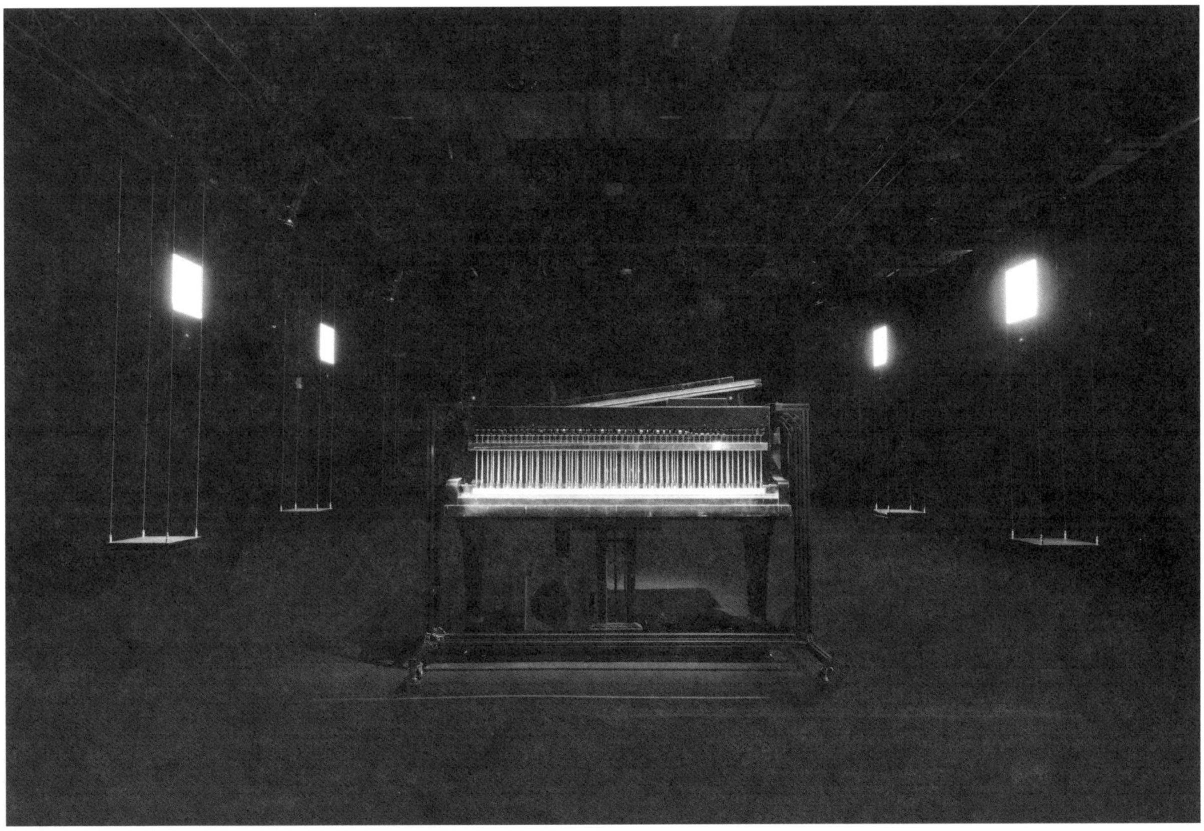

IS YOUR TIME | 2017
坂本龍一 with 高谷史郎
NTTインターコミュニケーション・センター［ICC］委嘱作品
台北流行音樂中心での展示風景（2021）© fundesign.tv

IS YOUR TIME | 2017
Ryuichi Sakamoto with Shiro Takatani
Commissioned by NTT InterCommunication Center [ICC]
Installation view at Taipei Music Center, 2021 © fundesign.tv

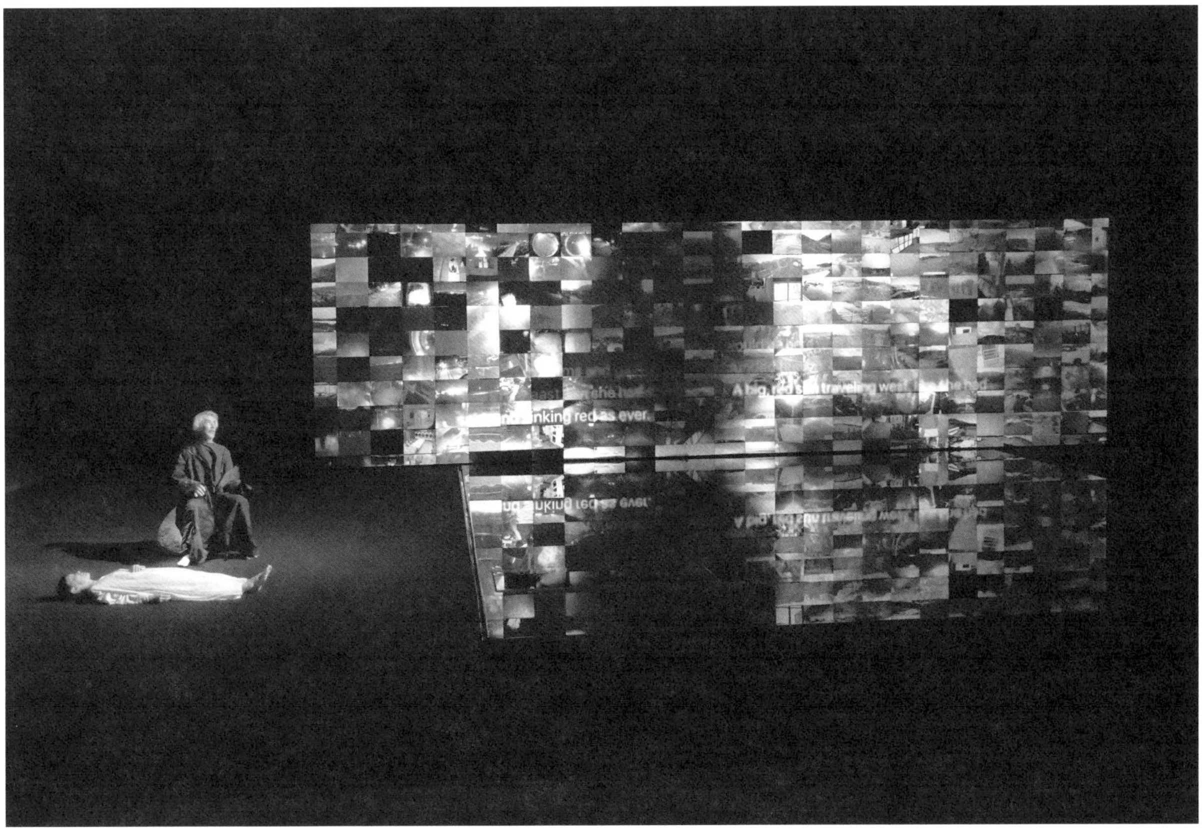

TIME | 2021
坂本龍一 ＋ 高谷史郎
出演：田中泯、宮田まゆみ
オランダ・フェスティバルにて世界初演
撮影：高谷桜子

TIME | 2021
Ryuichi Sakamoto + Shiro Takatani
with Min Tanaka, Mayumi Miyata
world premiere at Holland Festival
Photo: Yoko Takatani

ダムタイプ：
40年にわたり身体と形態をつなぐメディア

ダミアン・レンティーニ

ダムタイプは実に謎めいた存在である。1984年に芸術界への不満を抱え「ダムタイプ・シアター」を結成した京都市立芸術大学の学生たちは、視覚芸術、演劇、音楽、建築、グラフィックデザイン、アートプランニング、コンピューター・プログラミングなど多岐にわたる興味や専門領域において活動していた。そのため、グループの幅広い世界の一角をなす数々のサイドプロジェクトやコラボレーションは言うまでもなく、その多様な表現活動全体を正しく紹介するならば、パフォーマンス、メディアアート、インスタレーション、絵画、写真、映像といった多彩かつ相互に重なり合う分野の活動実績にも言及せねばならない。しかし、本稿においては、ダムタイプの活動を4つの特徴的な時代に分けて紹介したい。これらは重複する部分もあるが、それぞれ重要なプロジェクトや問題提起を行っており、そのなかには現在継続中のものもある。

第1期：喜び、人生、「バブル経済」

グループの結成に至る議論に参加していた学生の実際の数は定かではないが[*1]、一般にダムタイプは当初6名の「創設メンバー」で構成されたとみなされている。その6名とは古橋悌二、高谷史郎、小山田徹、穂積幸弘、藤本隆行、そして泊博雅[*2]である。創設メンバーの多くはもともと大学内の「劇団座カルマ」という演劇サークルに入っていたが、従来の演劇活動、さらには大学における指導の根幹にある師弟関係というものに不満を抱えていた。これを踏まえて、ダムタイプは当初から民主的な横割りの組織を構築し、メンバーそれぞれが新作の構想やデザインに関われるようにした。

*1 ——古橋悌二は以下のように語っている。「1984年、不満を抱え、アートを画廊や美術館の外に出したいと思っていた芸術科の学生約15名とダムタイプを始めました。みんなテクノロジーに興味を抱きつつも、情報時代幻想には疑問を感じていました。この二つのことが私たちを結びつけ、いまだに私たちの作品の核となっています」（キャロル・ラトフィ「The Conversation - Teiji Furuhashi」より。初出は『Tokyo Journal』1995年9月号［http://renfield.net/tj/9509/converse.html 最終アクセス日：2022年3月28日］。以下に再録：ダムタイプ編『メモランダム　古橋悌二』リトルモア、2000年、pp. 120–122）

*2 ——バーバラ・ロンドン「Teiji Furuhashi: Diamonds Are Forever」『ArtAsiaPacific』51号、2007年冬号、p. 95

グループの初期の活動で大きな支えになったのが、1980年代の京都における独特な文化シーン、そして日本の技術・経済成長が牽引した「バブル経済」末期に沸き起こった、未活用の新たな機会があるはずだという社会の意識だった。グループはそもそも活動を単なるパフォーマンスだけに絞ってはいなかったが、この2つの要素がグループ内に何物にもとらわれないチャレンジ精神を掻き立てることになり、古橋らが、スタンリー・キューブリック監督の映画『時計じかけのオレンジ』（1971）に登場する「コロヴァ・ミルク・バー」をモデルにした学生たちで運営するバー「ドラッグストア」で、定期的に実験映画や映像の上映会を開催するなどの活動につながった。実際、ダムタイプのメンバーの多くは早くからマルチメディア、特に映像と映画の分野で活躍していた。この時期、東京にあるビデオギャラリーSCANが極めて重要な役割を果たす。このギャラリーは後続に大きな影響を与えたパフォーマンス・アーティストで、「霧の彫刻家」として知られる中谷芙二子が主宰しており、こうした若い芸術家の多くに貴重な展示機会を与えていたのだ。このことは、古橋の初期の作品《7 Conversation Styles》（1984）が1985年「第1回東京国際ビデオ・ビエンナーレ」奨励賞を受賞し、翌年ニューヨーク近代美術館で開催された「New Video: Japan」展で上映されたことから明らかだ（映像を一部抜粋し、《Conversation Styles: Dumb Talk, Balance》として上映された）[*3]。この作品は19分のモノクロ映画で、「ダム」なロボット化した人間が「山」（実際は京都市動物園のサル舎）を背景によろめきまわる様子を古橋本人が演じ、のちにダムタイプの同時期のパフォーマンス作品で取り上げるテーマ

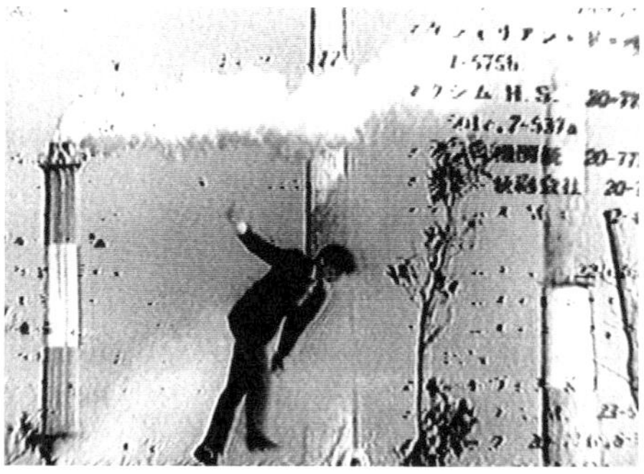

7 Conversation Styles, 1984

*3 ——バーバラ・ロンドン「New Video: Japan」展図録、アメリカ芸術連盟・ニューヨーク近代美術館、1986年、p. 16

やアイデアの多くに触れている。また、これが「愚か」、そして「口がきけない」という2つの意味を持つ「ダム（dumb）」という言葉をグループが使うきっかけとなった。

ダムタイプの初期のパフォーマンスやイベントは京都にあるアートスペース無門館という小劇場で行われた。そこで上演された作品には、《睡眠の計画#2》（1984）、《庭園の黄昏》（1985）、そして特筆すべきものに《036-Pleasure Life》（1987）がある。この作品は、グループが自身の名から「シアター」の文字を削った後初めて行われたパフォーマンスである。《036-Pleasure Life》、そして1988年に再アレンジして上演された《Pleasure Life》は、通常の演劇というよりはインスタレーションとパフォーマンスの融合といったほうがいい作品であるが、この時期までのダムタイプの活動を駆り立ててきたメインテーマにフォーカスしている。すなわち、あらゆるものに遍在すると言えるテクノロジーと情報のネットワークがもたらす、カラオケバーやファストフード店、有名人のトークショー番組を中心に回る生活との乖離である。この時代、日本の「ニュー・アカデミズム」と呼ばれた潮流、そして特に浅田彰によるポスト構造主義の哲学書で、高い人気を博した『構造と力』（1983）に影響を受けた理論的風潮が広く見られた。マリリン・アイビーの指摘によれば、浅田の著書はポストモダニズムを歴史と知識の「理想的限界」であると論じ、「リゾーム的で、散在的で、分散的で、多様性をもち、違いを容認するもの」こそ現代世界の意味を考察することを試みるにあたり、最も効果的な手段をなすとしている[*4]。この分散した思考をもとに、ダムタイプのプロジェクトのほとんどはインスタレーションやパフォーマンス、映像を融合して構成されており、その上（再）演のシチュエーションに合わせて常に一部だけ実施したり形態や内容を変えたりしている。これは《036-Pleasure Life》と《Pleasure Life》の2つのバージョンだけでなく、このプロジェクトのその後のアレンジとして制作され、1989年から91年にかけてアメリカ各地を巡回した「アゲインスト・ネイチャー　80年代の日本美術」展で展示されたインスタレーション《Playback》（1989）からも見て取れる。このインスタレーション作品は、両パフォーマンス作品の格子状に分割された舞台構成をそのまま採用しながら、《Pleasure Life》の重要な構成要素だった36脚のパイプ製の背の高い台座を25個のスチールとガラス製の台に置き換えたものだった。それぞれの台では、円形の蛍光灯と、透明なアクリル板がターンテーブルのように音もなく回っている（「ターンテーブル」にはトーンアームの代わりにプラスチック製のミサイルのようなオブジェが付いている）。その下に設置された蛍光灯がコンピューター制御で点滅し、回転する「レコード」に合わせて静かなリズムを刻む。

*4——マリリン・アイビー「Critical Texts, Mass Artifacts: The Consumption of Knowledge in Postmodern Japan」『Postmodernism and Japan』マサオ・ミヨシ、ハリー・ハルトゥーニアン、スタンリー・フィッシュ、フレドリック・ジェイムソン編、Duke University Press、1989年、p.29（以下にも引用されている：アレクサンドラ・モンロー「Hinomaru Illumination: Japanese Art of the 1990s」『Japanese Art After 1945. Scream Against the Sky』展図録、Harry N. Abrams、1994年、p.341）

第2期：「失われた数十年」

3つのエポックメイキングな出来事（2つは日本という国レベル、もう1つは個人レベル）がダムタイプの活動の第2期を形作っている。最初の2つの出来事は1989–90年に起こった。つまり、世界中で発生した、国際社会・政治に関する象徴的な出来事と同時代的に起こっていたわけだが、これらは日本の社会と政治に後戻りできない変革をもたらすこととなった。その1つ目が、1989年1月7日の昭和天皇の崩御による昭和時代の終焉。2つ目が同時期に起こった「バブル経済」の崩壊とそれに続くいわゆる「ロストジェネレーション」の幕開けである[*5]。キュレーターの吉竹美香は、このポスト昭和時代とその後の権力危機は数々の政治スキャンダルにまみれ、「ジェンダー問題、核の危機、ナショナリズム批判を、（中略）鋭いユーモアのセンスや政治問題への積極的な取り組みで知られるアーティストたちは特に痛感する」結果

*5——モンロー（1994、p.340）および、クリストファー・ウッド『The Bubble Economy: The Japanese Economic Collapse』Sidgwick & Jackson Ltd、1992年〔『バブル・エコノミー—日本経済・衰退か再生か』植山周一郎訳、共同通信社、1992年〕

になったと指摘する[*6]。こういったテーマはダムタイプのこの時期の2つの大きなプロジェクトに反映されている。両方とも、グループの活動が国際的に認められるようになった時期のものである。

この頃になるとパフォーマンス作品の規模も複雑さも大きく増し、ダムタイプは新作《pH》(1990)の初演を東京屈指の流行発信地・青山にあるアートスペース、スパイラルで行った。京都に本社を構える下着ブランド・ワコールが母体のアートセンターであるスパイラルがスポンサーを務め、ダムタイプが非常に高く評価されていたヨーロッパへの遠征費用を国際交流基金が担った[*7]。作品自体は細長い舞台とその上を絶えず行き来する2つの大きなトラスで構成されていた。2つのトラスのうち低いほうは床から数十センチしかなかった。このトラスが舞台上を横切るように移動するため、パフォーマーは常にこの低いバーに合わせて動かねばならない。下を這ってくぐったり上を飛び越えたり——。舞台の両側の目が眩むほど高い位置にある客席から眺める観客には、まるで巨大なコピー機やスキャナーに見えた。

《pH》から間もなく、ダムタイプは今もその代表作として名高い作品に着手する。《S/N》(1994)である。《S/N》というタイトルは音響用語で有効な信号(シグナル)と雑音(ノイズ)との量の比率を表す「S(信号)N(雑音)比」を意味する。このタイトルからわかる通り、《S/N》は性の不平等、人種・民族的少数者差別、障碍者差別、ジェンダー問題、HIV／エイズ、セクシュアリティなど現代社会が抱える諸問題を取り巻く不協和音を分析し、「パフォーマンスのみならず周囲の様々なコミュニティとの交流・連携といった具体的なアクティヴィズムまでも巻き込み展開された」[*8]。この最終到達点へ向けて、このプロジェクトの最初の2作品はLCDモニターやビデオプロジェクターを多用したミクストメディアのインスタレーションとして行われた[*9]。これらの作品の制作後、コペンハーゲンのホテル・プロ・フォルマとのコラボレーションに向けた準備中、古橋はグループのメンバーに手紙を書き、HIVに感染したことを告げた[*10]。この告白はグループに大きなショックを与え、古橋主導のパフォーマンス作品の制作が直ちに決められた。この作品ではまず、《S/Nの為のセミナー・ショー》(1993)と銘打った「パブリック・アウトリーチ(一般向け教育普及啓蒙)イベント」として、パフォーマーに加えゲストスピーカーも参加し、世界各国のHIV／エイズ啓発ポスターの紹介やセクシュアリティやジェンダーなどの「タブー」な話題を取り上げオープンに語り合うセッションを行った。観客の参加も可能で、むしろ積極的に勧められた。この「セミナー」、さらにマルチメディア・インスタレーションの成果として、1994年のアデレード・アートフェスティバルでパフォーマンス作品《S/N》が初演された[*11]。

実に多くの意味で、《S/N》はダムタイプの活動だけでなくパフォーマンスアートの歴史全体において象徴的な作品である。特筆すべきは、この作品がポスト昭和の日本だけでなく[*12]、いわゆるリベラルとされた西洋世界においても、あからさまに実行そして／または擁護する態度の中にみられるジェンダーやアイデンティティ、国籍に関する保守的な考え方に真っ向から挑んだことだ。この点において、《S/N》は過去の様々なパフォーマンスアートに加え非常にパーソナルなナラティヴを用い、壁を打ち払って舞台上だけで済ますことのできない逼迫した問題について観客に直に語りかけている[*13]。また、歌舞伎の女形から、古橋自身がニューヨークや大阪、東京で行っていたドラァグショーまで、パフォーマンスアートにおける異性装の伝統、さらに1980年代に京都市立芸術大学でグループメンバーの多くを指導した森村泰昌といったアーティストらによる同時期作品の手法を用いた。

こういった背景に加え、ピーター・エッカーソールはこの時期における、浅田

*6——吉竹美香「Parergon: Japanese Art of the 1980s and 1990s」展図録、Skira Editore、2019年、p.11

*7——ロンドン、2007年、p.96

*8——『DUMB TYPE 1984 2019』河出書房新社、2019年、pp.78–79

*9——シリーズ最初の作品《S/N#1》(1992)は横浜美術館、グッゲンハイム美術館ソーホー(ニューヨーク)、サンフランシスコ近代美術館を巡回した美術史上重要な展覧会である「戦後日本の前衛美術」展に出品された(アレクサンドラ・モンロー編「Japanese Art After 1945. Scream Against the Sky」展図録、Harry N. Abrams、1994年、p.358)

*10——藤本隆行「日本のマルチメディア・パフォーマンスを支える照明アーティスト藤本隆行の世界」『Performing Arts network Japan』国際交流基金、2009年7月31日(https://performingarts.jp/E/art_interview/0907/1.html. 最終アクセス日:2022年3月30日)

*11——しかしこれでプロジェクトは終了ではなく、CD(1995年リリース)や、ニューヨーク近代美術館に収蔵された《LOVERS》(1994)、さらに複数の作品に登場するインスタレーション《LOVE/SEX/DEATH/MONEY/LIFE》(1994)も制作された。

*12——竹田恵子によると、1993年時点でHIV感染者であることを公表した日本人男性は、古橋の他に2人しかいなかった。竹田恵子「Teiji Furuhashi: On 'Coming Out' in *S/N* (1994)」『The Dumb Type Reader』ピーター・エッカーソール、エドワード・シェアー、藤井慎太郎編、Museum Tusculanum Press、2017年、p.110

*13——これを最もよく表したのが、パフォーマンスの冒頭に古橋と他のパフォーマー2名が「male」「Japanese」「HIV+」「deaf」「American」「black」「homosexual」といった言葉が書かれたラベルが貼られたスーツを着て登場するシーンだろう。これらの言葉を人々に考えさせるのに劇場は適切な場かどうか議論したのち、古橋が「ここはシアターだから何が本当のことか誰もわからないよね?」と問いかけ、パフォーマーのピーター・ゴライトリーが突如英語で「I'm sorry to tell you, but we are not actors. We are this(申し訳ありませんが私たちは俳優ではありません。私たちはこれなのです)」と口上を述べ、最後に観客に対し「And, how are you?(それで皆さんは?)」と投げかけた。

の別の仕事の大きな影響を指摘している。1990年代に浅田が柄谷行人と共同編集した『批評空間』である[*14]。注目すべきは、『批評空間』が、ポストモダニズムの主要な論客らが議論を交わし、考えを広め、その後のアート、政治、社会へ影響を与えるプラットフォームとなったことだ。これにより、「失われた数十年」において主流だったポストモダンの実践に伴っていた落胆と鎮静に対抗するものとして、ハル・フォスターの提唱する「抵抗のポストモダニズム」が生まれた[*15]。

第3期：新たな千年紀／新たなメディア

1995年10月、古橋はエイズに起因する病によりこの世を去った。その死後、ダムタイプは喪の期間を経て、新たな千年紀への移行期に3作品で活動を再開する。この3作は過去のプロジェクト以上に、ダムタイプの美的・技術的工夫における転換点となったことを長谷川祐子は指摘している。「古橋亡き後、コンテンツ（ナラティヴ）は抽象化、断片化し、ナラティヴは音や光などのメディウム自体の増幅、変容といった、純度の高い身体感覚刺激のインターフェースに移行していった」[*16]。この点については高谷史郎と池田亮司による時に容赦なく迫りくる視覚・音響デザインによるところが大きい。高谷と池田は舞台に立つパフォーマーの身体と観客の身体の間にある種の一体感を作り上げようとしていたのだ。こういった、舞台装置を使って観客とパフォーマーの間につながりを生む試みは、《S/N》などの作品における対話によるつながりと明らかに対比されるだけでなく、ダムタイプが「ニューメディア・ドラマツルギー」なるものを、全作品にますます取り入れるようになったことを示すものである。ニューメディア・ドラマツルギーとは、端的に言えばパフォーマンスやインスタレーションの技術的要素を単なる補助装置と捉えるのではなく、むしろ「作品のドラマツルギーにおける主たる“役者”」とみなすアプローチである[*17]。パフォーマンスの「中」で実際に役をこなすものとして舞台装置を重視するこの手法は、前述の《pH》の動くトラスにもみられるが、それ以降の全プロジェクトで相当に強化されており、この3つのプロジェクトにおいては舞台上のパフォーマーと観客席の間のつながりをいっそう深めることに成功した。《OR》について高谷史郎はこう語っている。

> 「観客が体験する強烈な音と光は、舞台に立つ俳優やパフォーマーと観客の一体感をある種増幅させるものだと捉えています。演劇では観客は舞台上の俳優に感情移入しますが、テクノロジーは、舞台上の身体が経験するものを観客にも経験させ、それによりまた違った形でパフォーマーとの一体感を得ることで、その効果を増幅することができるのです」[*18]。

この「一体感の増幅」により、3つのプロジェクトはそれぞれが問題提起する異なる臨界状態において真に没入的な体験を作り出すことに成功している。《OR》(1997)のテーマである生と死の間にある「グレーゾーン」に始まり、これらの作品は記憶を辿ったり夢を見たりするなかで遭遇する空白（《memorandum》[1999]）、さらに地理的空間の位置を把握したり移動したりすることがもたらす認識の不一致（《Voyage》[2002]）を考察し、それにより観客に対し個人的感覚と普遍的感覚の間で常に揺れ動く体験をもたらした[*19]。

早逝した同志であり友への哀悼として、そして活動の抜本的な再編として、《OR》《memorandum》《Voyage》で生み出されたテクノロジーによる体験の増幅は、その後、数々のインタラクティブなインスタレーションや映像・

*14——ピーター・エッカーソール「Whiteout Dumb Type. Postmodernism and the Birth of New Media Dramaturgy」『The Dumb Type Reader』エッカーソール、エドワード・シェアー、藤井慎太郎編、Museum Tusculanum Press、2017年、p.163

*15——ピーター・エッカーソール（2017、p.163）、さらにハル・フォスター「序章」『反美学　ポストモダン文化の諸相』ハル・フォスター編、The New Press、1998年、xiii、〔『反美学　ポストモダンの諸相』室井尚・吉岡洋訳、勁草書房、1987年〕および、マサオ・ミヨシ・ハリー・ハルトゥーニアン「序章」『ポストモダニズムと日本』マサオ・ミヨシ・ハリー・ハルトゥーニアン編、Duke University Press、1989年、xi.

*16——長谷川祐子「The Dumb Type effect, 1984 to the present」『DUMB TYPE 1984 2019』河出書房新社、2019年、p.159

*17——ピーター・エッカーソール、ヘレナ・グレハン、エドワード・シェアー『New Media Dramaturgy: Performance, Media and New Materialism』Palgrave Macmillan、2017年、p.3

*18——高谷史郎へのインタビュー：エドワード・シェアー「Dumb Type's *XD*: A Case Study in New Media Dramaturgy」『The Dumb Type Reader』ピーター・エッカーソール、エドワード・シェアー、藤井慎太郎編、Museum Tusculanum Press、2017年、p.155

*19——芸術評論家の四方幸子は、「記憶そのものがインタラクティヴなものとして、つねに人間の知覚や身体を再編成することが示唆されている」と述べている。「〈イメージ=機械〉としての空間の行方」『ダムタイプ：ヴォヤージュ』展図録、NTT出版、2002年、p.30

パフォーマンス混成作品に引き継がれていく。これらはダムタイプのこれまでのどの作品よりも、我々の身体的経験、記憶、歴史はこの世界を構成するデジタルテクノロジーと切っても切れない関係であることを深く掘り下げている。しかし、この時代のいわゆる「ネオポップ」や「スーパーフラット」と呼ばれる世代[*20]のアーティストの多くとは対照的に、これらのプロジェクトはいずれも現代テクノロジーの遍在性に関してはシニカルでも過剰にディストピアンでもなく、むしろあらゆる技術的発展がいかに必然的に個人とその周りの世界の関係性をラディカルに再構築することにつながっているかを示している。

*20——「ネオポップ」は「ストリートカルチャー、マンガ、アニメなどの幅広いサブカルチャーを巧みに活用しながら、モダニスト的な上下階級を覆した1990年代を通して活躍したアーティスト世代を特徴とし、のちに村上隆が「スーパーフラット」と名づけた」(訳は本書による)ものと吉竹は定義している。吉竹美香「Parergon: Japanese Art of the 1980s and 1990s」展図録(Skira Editore、2019年、p.11)、村上隆「スーパーフラット」展図録(マドラ出版、2000年)および、村上隆編『リトルボーイ—爆発する日本のサブカルチャー・アート』(ジャパン・ソサエティー、イェール大学出版局、2005年)を参照。

第4期:アクション+リフレクションとその後

《Voyage》の最終公演(2009年カンヌ公演)の後、5年間はダムタイプにとって活動休止ともいえる期間となり、メンバーはそれぞれ新たなコラボレーションやアーティスト集団へと別々の道を歩んだ。池田亮司や高谷史郎などはソロで活躍し、特に高谷は中谷芙二子や田中泯、坂本龍一などと数々のサイトスペシフィック作品のコラボレーションを行っている。

そして2014年、ダムタイプのもとに東京都現代美術館でキュレーターを務めていた長谷川祐子から、「新たな系譜学をもとめて——跳躍/痕跡/身体」展のために新作の制作が打診される。その結果生まれたのが、マルチチャンネル・インスタレーション《MEMORANDUM OR VOYAGE》(2014)である。これは前述の3つのパフォーマンス作品とそれに付随して制作されたインスタレーションの要素で構成されている。この展覧会での展示、さらにポンピドゥー・センター・メッス(2018)、東京都現代美術館(2019–2020)、そしてミュンヘンのハウス・デア・クンスト(2022)での展示はダムタイプにとってその多様なプロジェクトを展開し続け、新しい構成に挑戦するきっかけとなった。その例が古舘健や濱哲史、白木良といったプログラマーとのコラボレーションである。直近では、坂本龍一とともに16都市から集めたフィールド・レコーディング音源を使用して《Playback》用の新たな音源を制作しており、この作品の続きはヴェネチアの日本館で聴くことができる。《Playback》は元をたどれば先に紹介した1987年のパフォーマンス作品《036-Pleasure Life》まで遡り、まさに、ダムタイプがいかに常に形を定めず様々な状況に適応して活動してきたかを示す最高の例だろう。また、前述のリゾーム的なもののように、このプロジェクト自体がダムタイプならではの多元的な世界において、今後さらなる表現を繰り返していく際の中心点となるであろうことは想像に難くない。

(ハウス・デア・クンスト キュレーター)

Dumb Type: (Media)ting of Bodies and Forms Across Four Decades

Damian Lentini

Dumb Type are a true enigma. In keeping with the diverse interests and disciplines that informed the group of disaffected students from Kyoto City University of the Arts who came together to form Dumb Type Theater in 1984—which included visual arts, theatre, music, architecture, graphic design, arts planning and computer programming—a proper overview of the group's multivalent practice, not to mention the myriad of side projects and collaborations that are no less part of their expanded universe, must include the variegated and overlapping histories of performance, theatre, media art, installation, painting, photography and film. However, for the purposes of this essay, Dumb Type's practice will be divided into four distinct, yet overlapping periods, each of which produced several major projects and lines of enquiry; some of which continue today.

First phase: Pleasure, Life and the "Bubble Economy"

Although there is some conjecture about the exact number of students who participated in the group's early discussions,[*1] Dumb Type is commonly seen as originally comprising six "founding members": Teiji Furuhashi, Shiro Takatani, Toru Koyamada, Yukihiro Hozumi, Takayuki Fujimoto and Hiromasa Tomari.[*2] Many of these founding members were originally part of the University's theatre company Gekidan za-Karma, but were nonetheless unhappy with the master/apprentice relationship that underpinned both traditional theatre practice, as well as the teaching at the University. With this in mind, Dumb Type instigated a democratic, horizontal operational structure from the outset, in which every member was able to contribute to the conceptualisation and design of new projects.

*1 — As Teiji Furuhashi recounts: "I started dumb type in 1984 with about 15 other frustrated art students who wanted to take art outside galleries and museums. We were all interested in technology, but suspicious of the information-age dream. Those two things bonded us together and are still vital to our work today" (Carol Lutfy, "The Conversation—Teiji Furuhashi," first published in *Tokyo Journal,* September 1995, http://renfield.net/tj/9509/converse.html, last accessed 28 March, 2022); subsequently reprinted in Dumb Type (ed.) *memorandum teiji furuhashi*, Tokyo: Little More, 2000: 123.

*2 — Barbara London, "Teiji Furuhashi. Diamonds Are Forever," *ArtAsiaPacific*, 51, Winter 2007: 95.

Greatly benefitting the group's initial work was the unique cultural scene of Kyoto during the 1980s, as well as sense of untapped opportunities that accompanied the final years of Japan's tech- and finance-driven "bubble economy." These two factors contributed to an air of almost unbounded experimentation from within the group—who, from the outset, never confined their practice to simply performance—and allowed, for example, Furuhashi and others to regularly curate evenings of experimental film and video at the student-run bar Drugstore; a club modelled on the Korova Milk Bar of Kubrick's "Clockwork Orange." Indeed, early on, many members of Dumb Type found success working across multiple media, but especially video and film. Here, the Tokyo-based Video Gallery SCAN, founded in 1980 by the seminal performance artist and fog sculptor Fujiko Nakaya, would play a pivotal role, providing many of these still young artists with invaluable exhibition opportunities. This is evidenced by an early work of Furuhashi, *7 Conversation Styles* (1984), winning an award at the 1985 Tokyo International Video Biennale; an excerpted version of which—entitled *Conversation Styles: Dumb Talk, Balance*—was subsequently included as part of the exhibition "New Video: Japan" that was shown at New York's Museum of Modern Art the following year.[*3] The work itself, a nineteen minute black and white film in which Furuhashi plays a "dumb" robotised everyman stumbling about against the backdrop of a "mountain"—actually the monkey house of Kyoto Zoo—would touch on many of these themes and ideas that would later be taken up in Dumb Type's concurrent performance work; as well as signal the group's use of the double meaning of the word "dumb" English as both "stupid" and being rendered "speechless."

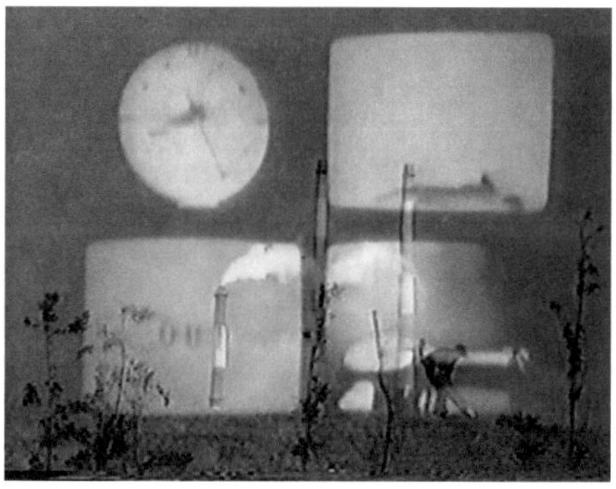

7 Conversation Styles, 1984

*3 — Barbara London, *New Video: Japan*, exh. cat., New York: American Federation of Arts and Museum of Modern Art, 1986: 16.

Dumb Type staged many of their early performances and events in a small theatre space called the Artspace Mumonkan in Kyoto. These included *Plan for Sleep #2* (1984), *Every Dog Has His Day* (1985) and, most importantly, *036-Pleasure Life* (1987); which signalled the first performance undertaken after it was decided to drop the word "Theater" from their title. Far more akin to a hybrid installation/performance than a straight up work of theatre, *036-Pleasure Life*—and its subsequent reimagining as *Pleasure Life* in 1988—focused in on many of the key themes that had driven Dumb Type's work up until this period: the detachment of a life based around karaoke bars, fast food restaurants and celebrity talk shows; all mediated by an almost ubiquitous network of technology and information. Here, one detects that pervasive theoretical influence of what was termed "new academism" in Japan and especially of Akira Asada's incredibly popular poststructuralist text *Structure and Power* (*Kōzō to chikara*, 1983). According to Marilyn Ivy, Asada's text posited postmodernism as the "ideal limit" of history and knowledge, positing that the "rhizomatic, the disseminated, the dispersed, and the multiple—that which is affirmative of difference" constituted the most effective means through which we can attempt to make sense of the contemporary world.[*4] In keeping with this dispersed mode of thinking, almost all of Dumb Type's projects would comprise a mixture of installation, performance and video, and would continually branch off and readapt both their form and the content in response the situations underpinning their (re)presentation. This was not only evident in the two different manifestations of *036-Pleasure Life* / *Pleasure Life*, but also in the project's subsequent reimagining as the installation *Playback* (1989) that formed part of the exhibition "Against Nature: Japanese Art in the Eighties" that toured the United States in 1989–1991. This installation maintained the grid formation of both performances, but replaced the thirty-six wire plinths that were the key organisational element of *Pleasure Life* with twenty-five steel-and-glass stands, each supporting a circular fluorescent light and a turntable-like structure upon which a transparent acrylic plate spun soundlessly (in place of the tone arm, the "turntable" instead bore a plastic missile-like object). A computer program controlled the sequence of lights under the "turntables," turning them on and off to generate a sort of silent rhythm to accompany the spinning "records."

*4 — Marilyn Ivy, "Critical Texts, Mass Artifacts: The Consumption of Knowledge in Postmodern Japan" in Masao Miyoshi, Harry Harootunian, Stanley Fish and Fredric Jameson (eds.) *Postmodernism and Japan*, New York, USA: Duke University Press, 1989: 29; cited in Alexandra Munroe, "Hinomaru Illumination: Japanese Art of the 1990s" in *Japanese Art After 1945. Scream Against the Sky*, exh. cat., New York: Harry N. Abrams Inc. 1994: 341.

Second phase: The "Lost Decades"

Three epochal events—two national and one deeply personal—would frame Dumb Type's second major period of work. The first two of these would take place in period 1989–1990—that is, concurrent with similarly paradigmatic global and political events throughout the world—and would amount to an irretrievable restructuring of Japanese society and politics. The first of these was the passing of Emperor Hirohito and the subsequent end of the Showa era on 7 January 1989; while the second was the concurrent collapse of the "bubble economy" and the subsequent beginning of the so-called lost generation(s).[*5] According to the curator Mika Yoshitake, this post-Showa era and the subsequent crisis of authority ushered in by a series of political scandals resulted in a scene in which "politics of gender, nuclear crisis, and critiques of nationalism [...] were especially poignant amongst artists [...] who were all known for their sharp sense of humour and active engagement with political issues."[*6] These themes were in turn mirrored by Dumb Type's two major projects from this period; both of which coincided with a period of major international recognition for their practice.

*5 — Munroe, 1994: 340. See also Christopher Wood, *The Bubble Economy: The Japanese Economic Collapse*, London: Sidgwick and Jackson, 1992.

*6 — Mika Yoshitake, *Parergon: Japanese Art of the 1980s and 1990s*, exh. cat., Milan: Skira Editore, 2019: 11.

In keeping with the significant increase in both scale and complexity of their performance practice, Dumb Type premiered their new production, *pH* (1990) at the multipurpose art space Spiral in Tokyo's fashionable Aoyama district. The Kyoto-based lingerie company Wacoal—who also owned Spiral—sponsored the work, while the Japan Foundation covered the costs of shipping the production to Europe, where the group found an extremely appreciative audience.[*7] The work itself comprised of an elongated thrust stage, along which two large truss bars continually shifted back and forth; the lower of which was only a few feet from the floor. As a result of the sweeping movements, performers were constantly having to negotiate the low scanning bar—either by crawling underneath or leaping over the top of it as it made yet another pass along the stage—which for the audience, who were vertiginously seated on either side of the stage, resembled a giant photocopier or scanner.

Not long after *pH*, Dumb Type commenced work on what would be their most famous project to date: *S/N* (1994). As indicated by the title—which in audio terminology stands for "signal/noise" (signal-to-noise ratio), a scale that determines the relative amount of effective versus extraneous information contained within a coded message—*S/N* constituted a study into the dissonance surrounding a swath of contemporary social issues (sex inequality, racial and ethnic minority discrimination, ableism, politics of gender, HIV/AIDS and sexualities) "in an effort to go beyond the theatrics of art towards activist engagement and community outreach."[*8] To this end, the first two manifestations of the project were mixed media installations that comprised a series of LCD monitors and video projectors.[*9] Subsequent to the creation of these works—and while they were preparing for a collaboration with Hotel Pro Forma in Copenhagen—Furuhashi wrote a letter to each member of the group and revealed that he had tested HIV positive.[*10] Such was the impact of this announcement, it was immediately decided to create a performance work, primarily driven by Furuhashi. This first took the form of the *Seminar Show for S/N* (1993), a "public outreach event" which featured performers, guest speakers, a presentation of international HIV/AIDS awareness posters and an open conversation covering sexuality, gender and other "taboo" subjects; audience participation was both possible and actively encouraged. The performance *S/N*—which was the result of both this "seminar," as well as the multimedia installations—then premiered at the Adelaide Arts Festival in 1994.[*11]

In so many ways, *S/N* constitutes a paradigmatic moment both within Dumb Type's specific practice and within the wider history of performance. Importantly, the work directly confronted conservative politics pertaining to gender, identity and nationality not just with respect to post-Showa-Japan,[*12] but also with respect to the overtly exercised and/or patronising attitudes on display within the so-called liberal West. In this regard, *S/N* drew upon both wider histories of performance and deeply personal narratives; constantly breaking the fourth wall and speaking directly to the audience about matters that were far too urgent to leave simply on stage.[*13] Other segments draw upon the tradition of cross-dressing in performance—from the gender transformation undertaken by *Onnagata* in Kabuki theatre, to Furuhashi's own experiences performing in drag shows in New York, Osaka and Tokyo—as well as the contemporaneous work of artists such as Yasumasa Morimura; who had taught many of them at Kyoto City University of the Arts in the 1980s.

In addition to these specific histories, Peter Eckersall points to the profound influence of another of Asada's projects during this period: the journal *Critical Space* (*Hihyōkūkan*) that Asada co-edited with Karatani Kōjin in the 1990s.[*14] Importantly, *Critical Space* offered a platform for debate and dissemination of many of the major theoreticians of postmodernism and its subsequent impact on art, politics and society; allowing for the development of what Hal Foster has termed a "postmodernism of resistance" that opposed the

*7 — London, 2007: 96.

*8 — *Dumb Type 1984 2019*, Tokyo: Kawade Shobo Shinsha Ltd., 2019: 79.

*9 — The first work, *S/N #1* (1992), was included as part of the landmark exhibition *Scream Against the Sky* that toured the Yokohama Museum of Art, Guggenheim Museum SoHo New York, and the San Francisco Museum of Modern Art (Alexandra Munroe (ed.), *Japanese Art After 1945: Scream Against the Sky*, exh. cat., New York: Harry N. Abrams, Inc., 1994: 358.

*10 — Takayuki Fujimoto, "The world of Takayuki Fujimoto, a lighting artist at the forefront in Japan's multimedia performance scene," *Performing Arts Network Japan*, The Japan Foundation, 31 July, 2009 (https://performingarts.jp/E/art_interview/0907/1.html, last accessed 30 March, 2022).

*11 — However, this did not signal the end of the project, as the performance then generated both a CD (1995), as well as two new installations: *Lovers* (1994), which was acquired by New York's Museum of Modern Art; as well as *LOVE/SEX/DEATH/MONEY/LIFE* (1994), an installation that has appeared in multiple manifestations.

*12 — According to Keiko Takeda, as of 1993 there were only two other Japanese males besides Furuhashi who had publicly disclosed that they had HIV. Keiko Takeda, "Teiji Furuhashi: On 'Coming Out' in S/N (1994)," in *The Dumb Type Reader*, ed. Peter Eckersall, Edward Scheer, Fujii Shintaro, Copenhagen: DK, Museum Tusculanum Press, 2017: 110.

*13 — This is perhaps best exemplified at the very beginning of the performance, when Furuhashi and two other performers emerge wearing suits upon which several labels bearing a selection of the words "male," "Japanese," "HIV+," "deaf," "American," "black" and "homosexual" are written. After discussing whether the theatre is an appropriate place to make people aware of these labels—at one point, Furuhashi asks, "this is theatre, so who's sure what's real or not?"—the performer Peter Golightly suddenly switches to English and announces "I'm sorry to tell you, but we are not actors. We are this," before finishing by asking the audience "And, how are you?"

*14 — Peter Eckersall, "Whiteout Dumb Type: Postmodernism and the Birth of New Media Dramaturgy," in *The Dumb Type Reader*, ed. Peter Eckersall, Edward Scheer, Fujii Shintaro, Copenhagen: DK, Museum Tusculanum Press, 2017: 163.

atmosphere of despondency and pacification that was associated with mainstream postmodern practices during the "lost decades."*[15]

Third phase: New Millennium/New Media

After Furuhashi tragically died of an AIDS-related illness in October 1995, Dumb Type undertook a period of mourning, before returning with a trilogy of projects around the turn of the new millennium. More so than their previous projects, Yuko Hasegawa has noted how these three works in particular signalled a turning point in the aesthetic and technological strategies deployed by Dumb Type: "After Furuhashi's death, the content (narrative) of their work became more abstract and fragmentary: it shifted toward an interface of stimuli that provoked various pure, physical sensations. The media themselves, such as the sound and light, became amplified and transformed."*[16] Much of the credit in this regard was paid to by the at-times unrelenting visual and sonic designs of Shiro Takatani and Ryoji Ikeda, who sought to create a sort of identification between the bodies of the performers on stage with those in the audience. This notion of using the mise-en-scene to establish a form of connection between audience and performer obviously contrasts with the more dialogue-driven connection established by works such as *S/N*, but also importantly demonstrates Dumb Type's increasing embrace of what has been termed "New Media Dramaturgy" within all of their work. In short, New Media Dramaturgy does not consider the technical elements of a performance or installation as merely ancillary, but rather "as key *players* in each work's dramaturgy."*[17] This emphasis on the mise-en-scene as an actual determining participant *within* a performance—as seen in the aforementioned example of the moving truss bar in *pH*, but strengthened significantly in every project since—allowed for this trilogy of projects to in turn intensify the connection between the performers on stage and those sitting in the audience. As Shiro Takantani noted with respect to *OR*:

> The violence of the sound and the light that the audience can experience is for me a kind of amplification of the identification of the audience with the actor or performer on stage. In theatre, the audience identifies with the actors on stage but the technology can help by amplifying this effect, by making the audience experience these things that the body on stage also experiences, and in that way also identify with the performer in a different, additional way.*[18]

Via this "amplification of the identification," these three projects were in turn able to generate truly immersive experiences within their interrogations of different modes of liminality. Beginning with the "grey zone" between life and death that was explored with *OR* (1997), the works went on to investigate the lacunae encountered within the act of recalling or dreaming (*memorandum*, 1999) and, finally, the gaps in knowledge brought about by our attempts to map and traverse geographic spaces (*Voyage*, 2002); in turn generating experiences for the audience that continually shifted between the personal and the universal.*[19]

As a form of both collective mourning for their departed colleague and friend, as well as a radical reconfiguration of their practice, this tech-driven amplification of experience generated by *OR, memorandum* and *Voyage* was then carried over into a series of interactive installations and video/performance hybrids that probed deeper than perhaps any of Dumb Type's previous works the ways in which the experiences of our bodies, memories and our histories are in fact indissoluble from the digital technologies through which we organise our worlds. However, in contrast to many of the concurrent artists of the so-called

*15 — Eckersall, 2017: 163. See also Hal Foster, "Introduction" in *The Anti-Aesthetic: Essays on Postmodern Culture*, ed. Hal Foster, New York: The New Press, 1998: xiii; and Masao Miyoshi and Harry Harootunian, "Introduction" in *Postmodernism and Japan*, eds. Masao Miyoshi and Harry Harootunian, Durham and London: Duke University Press, 1989: xi.

*16 — Yuko Hasegawa "The Dumb Type Effect, 1984 to the Present" in *Dumb Type 1984 2019*, Tokyo: Kawade Shobo Shinsha Ltd., 2019: 170.

*17 — Peter Eckersall, Helena Grehan and Edward Scheer, *New Media Dramaturgy: Performance, Media and New Materialism*, London: Palgrave Macmillan, 2017: 3 (emphasis in original text).

*18 — Interview with Shiro Takatani, cited in Edward Scheer, "Dumb Type's *XD*: A Case Study in New Media Dramaturgy," in Peter Eckersall, Edward Scheer, Fujii Shintaro (eds.) *The Dumb Type Reader*, Copenhagen: DK, Museum Tusculanum Press, 2017: 155.

*19 — As the art critic Yukiko Shikata notes, "memory itself constantly reconfigures human perception and the body, as an interactive entity." ("Space as 'Image-Machine'" in *dumb type: Voyages*, Tokyo: NTT InterCommunication Center [ICC], 2002: 30)

*20 — Yoshitake defines "Neo-Pop" as "characterised by a generation of artists active throughout the 1990s who playfully appropriated a wide range of subcultures spanning street culture, manga, anime, while upending the modernist hierarchies of high and low—retroactively dubbed "superflat" by Takashi Murakami." (Mika Yoshitake, *Parergon: Japanese Art of the 1980s and 1990s*, (exh. cat.), Milan: Skira Editore, 2019: 11—see also Takashi Murakami, *Superflat*, (exh. cat.), Tokyo: Madra Publishing Co., 2000; Takashi Murakami (ed.), *Little Boy: The Arts of Japan's Exploding Subculture*, New York: Japan Society; New Haven and London: Yale University Press, 2005)

Neo-Pop or Superflat generation,*20 none of these projects could be described as either cynical or overtly dystopian with respect to the ubiquity of contemporary technologies, but rather signalled the manner in which all forms of technological developments necessarily result in a radical re-collaboration of the relationship between individuals and the world around them.

Fourth phase: Actions + Reflections and beyond

The five years subsequent to the last performance of *Voyage* (in Cannes, France in 2009) represented something of a sabbatical for Dumb Type; with each member branching off into new collaborations and artist constellations. Artists such as Ryoji Ikeda and Shiro Takatani, for example, would develop significant solo careers, with the latter also undertaking a series of important site-specific collaborations with artists such as Fujiko Nakaya, Min Tanaka and Ryuichi Sakamoto.

Then in 2014, Dumb Type were approached by Yuko Hasegawa, curator of the Museum of Contemporary Art Tokyo, and invited to create a new work for the exhibition "Seeking New Genealogies—Bodies / Leaps / Traces." This resulted in the multichannel installation *MEMORANDUM OR VOYAGE* (2014), which combined elements of all three of the aforementioned performances, as well as their subsequent installations. This show, as well as their important exhibitions at Centre Pompidou-Metz (2018), Museum of Contemporary Art Tokyo (2019–20) and Munich's Haus der Kunst (2022) have allowed Dumb Type to continue to develop many of their various project threads, as well as to work within new configurations; such as their collaborations with programmers such as Ken Furudate, Satoshi Hama and Ryo Shiraki. Most recently, they have also worked closely with Ryuichi Sakamoto on a new sound composition for the work *Playback*, featuring field recordings taken from sixteen different cities; a further manifestation of which can also be experienced in the pavilion in Venice. Indeed, there could hardly be a better example of the highly adaptive, amorphous manner in which Dumb Type have always worked than this particular installation, whose origins, as mentioned previously, can be traced all the way back to the 1987 performance *036-Pleasure Life.* And indeed, much like the rhizome alluded to above, one could well imagine that this project could itself act as its own nodal point for future iterations within Dumb Type's own unique multiverse.

(Curator of Haus der Kunst, Munich)

展覧会レビュー1
Review 1

ダムタイプ：超人間主義《トランスヒューマニズム》の時代におけるpost-truth

ダニエレ・ペラ

「ダムタイプはシステムである。活動開始以来、特定のディレクターを置かず、様々なメンバーが参加し、フラットな関係での共同制作を行い、その活動の領域を拡張してきた。ダムタイプは、さらに拡張する。ダムタイプは、観察する――自然を、テクノロジーを、社会を、人間を、post-truthの時代を。今まで信じてきたシステムが崩壊しようとしている分断された混沌しかない世界で、今まで事実だと思われていたものが不確かに感じられ、人々は自分たちが信じたいものを『真実』と思い込む」。

しかし、「post-truth」とはいったい何なのか？　作家リー・マッキンタイアは「事実が政治的視点に従属すること」と定義している。著書『POST TRUTH』（MIT出版[*1]）で、マッキンタイアは近年の事例を分析し、「post-truthとは証拠に関係なく誰かに何かを信じさせようとするイデオロギーの優位性を主張する手段」だと結論付けた。従来のメディアが衰退し、ソーシャルメディアが台頭してフェイクニュースが危険な政治的道具にされる時代において、人はpost-truthに対抗することができ、その最初の一歩はpost-truthを理解することであると、マッキンタイアは説いている。これこそ、ダムタイプが目指すものなのだろう。ダムタイプは1984年京都で結成し日本を拠点に活動するマルチメディア・アート・コレクティヴだ。彼らは複数の媒体を通じ、テクノロジーの役割、そして我々の生きる社会と環境に対し深く問いかけている。ヴィジュアル・アート、ビデオ、コンピューター・プログラミング、音楽、ダンスなど多彩な分野から集まった複数のアーティストで構成され、40年近くにもわたって集団による共同制作の可能性を探る独自の活動を続けてきたマルチメディア集団であり、その根幹にはプロジェクト毎に参加メンバーが変わる、ヒエラルキーのないコラボレーションがある。ダムタイプの作品はメルボルン国際アートフェスティバル、バービカン・センター（ロンドン）、新国立劇場（東京）、国際モダンダンス・フェスティバル（ソウル）、リヨン現代美術館、アテネ・コンサートホール、シンガポール芸術祭、シカゴ現代美術館、アムステルダム市立劇場など、世界中数多くの会場で上演・展示されている。

ダムタイプのステートメントは次のとおり。「『真実』は、もはやかつての『真実』ではない。『未来』は、もはやかつての『未来』ではない。『希望』は、もはやかつての『希望』ではない。『幸せ』は、もはやかつての『幸せ』ではない。インターネット上の言説空間＝post-truthをどう受け止め、霧のように重さのなくなった言葉に包囲されている情報環境の中で『当たり前』を純粋な視線で見つめ直し、『今をどう理解し、生き、そして死んでいくのか？』を問い続けなければならない」。ヴェネチア・ビエンナーレに日本から参加するグループメンバーは、高谷史郎、坂本龍一、古舘健、濱哲史、白木良、原摩利彦、泊博雅、南琢也、高谷桜子他。国際交流基金がコミッショナーを務める今回発表された新作は、北東南西の方角に置かれた4台の高速で回転する鏡にレーザーを反射させて、周囲の壁に文字を投影する。

1850年代の地理の教科書から引用されたテキストが、シンプルで普遍的な問いを投げかける。回転する超指向性スピーカーからテキストを朗読する音声が流れている。周囲を取り囲む言説群と対比的に、部屋の中央には空白の場所がある――「それはどこでもない場所であり、どこでもある場所である。我々は『Post Truth』『Liminal Spaces』の時代に生きている」。複雑で没入感溢れるマルチメディア・インスタレーションの今作は、人類の未来、そして何が「真」の真実なのか理解する力について重大な問いを投げかけている。だが、真の真実というものはそもそもあったのだろうか？　これからも信じていくべき真実とは何なのだろうか？

---

*1――翻訳書は「ポストトゥルース」大橋完太郎監修、居村匠・大﨑智史・西橋卓也訳、人文書院、2020年刊行。

初出：『exibart』紙（2022年4月／6月号、No.116）

Dumb Type: post-truth in the era of Transhumanism

Daniele Perra

"Dumb Type is a system. Since our founding we have welcomed the participation of various members, engaging in collaborations through a non-hierarchical relationship without a typical director figure. Dumb Type continues to further expand, turning an observant eye to nature, technology, society, human beings and the era of post-truth. In a world of fragmented chaos in which the systems we believed in are on verge of collapse, what had once appeared to be fact now seems uncertain, and people assume what they want to believe in as being the 'truth'."

But what, exactly, is post-truth? Author Lee McIntyre defines it as the "political subordination of reality." In his book *Post-Truth*, published by MIT Press, he analyzed recent examples and found that "post-truth is an assertion of ideological supremacy by which its practitioners try to compel someone to believe something regardless of the evidence." In a time when traditional media decline, social media rise, and fake news turn to be dangerous political tools, McIntyre argues that we can fight post-truth, and that the first step in fighting post-truth is to understand it. This is probably what the Japan-based artistic multimedia collective Dumb Type, founded in Kyoto 1984, wants to achieve. Through several interventions, the group is deeply questioning the role of technology, society and the nature we all live in. Composed of artists from various backgrounds including visual arts, video, computer programming, music, and dance, for nearly 40 years, the multimedia group has constantly explored the possibilities of collective collaboration through an array of distinctive projects. Its practice has been based on non-hierarchic collaborations in which participating members change according to specific projects. Their works have been performed and exhibited in numerous international venues including the Melbourne International Arts Festival, The Barbican Centre (London), New National Theatre (Tokyo), International Modern Dance Festival (Seoul), Musee d'art contemporain de Lyon, The Athens Concert Hall, Singapore Arts Festival, Museum of Contemporary Art Chicago, and Stadsschouwburg Amsterdam.

Dumb Type stated: "the 'truth' is no longer 'truth' as it used to be. The 'future' is no longer the 'future' as it used to be. 'Hope' is no longer 'hope' as it used to be. 'Happiness' is no longer 'Happiness' as it used to be. We must continue to question how to perceive spaces of discourse on the internet = post-truth, and ask ourselves 'How should we understand the present, live our lives, and die?' while revisiting 'norms' through a pure and unfaltering gaze in the context of an information environment where words are like fog and have lost their weight." Among the group's members to represent Japan at the Venice Biennale are: Shiro TAKATANI, Ryuichi SAKAMOTO, Ken FURUDATE, Satoshi HAMA, Ryo SHIRAKI, Marihiko HARA, Hiromasa TOMARI, Takuya MINAMI and Yoko TAKATANI. Their new environmental work, commissioned by the Japan Foundation, is composed of several mirrors on four stands that rotate at high speed, reflecting lasers trained on them to project text onto the walls.

The texts are taken from an 1850s geography textbook, posing basic yet universal questions. The sounds of voices reading the texts are emitted from rotating speakers. In contrast to the discourses that surround it, the center of the room is an empty space—"a place that exists nowhere, but at the same time a place that could be anywhere. We live in a time of post-truth and liminal spaces. The center is void." This new complex immersive multimedia installation raises crucial questions on the future of human beings and their capacity to understand what the "true" truth is. But has there ever been a true truth? What is the truth we should still believe in?

This text was published on *exibart*, no 116, April/June, 2022

展覧会レビュー2
Review 2

ヴェネチア・ビエンナーレ日本館

ダムタイプ、ジオグラフィー(地理)はヒエラルキーなく問いかける

ロッセッラ・メネガッツォ

ダムタイプ「2022」。1984年に京都で高谷史郎(1963-)、古橋悌二(1960-1995)らにより結成されたこの日本のアーティスト・コレクティヴは、1980-90年代の経済バブル期にテクノロジーを駆使した彼らのパフォーマンスに出会った、前衛的かつ実験的な日本を愛する多くの熱狂的ファンにとっては、その名前を目にするだけで郷愁、感動、興奮が呼び起こされるような存在だ。その名前自体が形式とヒエラルキーの解体という彼らの意志を表しており、プロジェクトに合わせてメンバーは変化し、その数が増減するのみならず、プロジェクトそのものが民主的創造性の産物である。幾夜も議論を重ね、それぞれが自由に意見を出し合うことで、常に変化するインスタレーションやパフォーマンスが形づくられる。そこではアーティストや科学者の専門性が交差する。

2022年の日本館では、10人のメンバーが参加し、グループの円熟を感じさせるものであった。高谷史郎、著名な音楽家、作曲家である坂本龍一——彼は来月5月にミュンヘンのハウス・デア・クンストで開催される展覧会で展示予定のインスタレーション《Playback》のために録音されたサウンドトラックも提供している——、古舘健、濱哲史、白木良、原摩利彦、泊博雅、南琢也、空里香、高谷桜子。その他に、坂本と親交のあるアーティストら16人が、世界中の異なる都市で街の音を録音した。そして暗い館内に設置された回転式の超指向性スピーカーから流れるこのサウンドが、1時間にわたり観衆を異次元の地平へと誘う。館内の壁面には、赤いレーザー光線と白い帯やスポットの光線とが交互に投影される。5本の水平なラインで、時にはシグナル、時にはテキストが映し出される。子供の「なぜ?」についての本、あるいは教科書に見られるような短い疑問文。「火山はどこから生まれるの?」「海はいくつある?」「川って何?」といった問いかけは、自然や地理に関わる現象の起源についての普遍的な疑問を想起させる。興味深いのは、これらの問いかけが、今日のような観察や分析技術(航空写真や宇宙探査といった地球の全容を理解できる技術)が存在せず、地球や宇宙に関する知識が乏しい1850年代にアメリカで出版された地理の教科書から選ばれたことだろう。この場合にはアメリカだが、そうした地域的な特性を排除すると、これらの疑問は世界中のどの教科書でも共通であるように思われ、国や国境、我々と世界との関係といった概念について考察させてくれる。

テキストは流れゆく雲の映像と交互に映し出される。5本のラインにピクセルで分割され、水面に映し出される風景のようにぼんやりと見える効果が付されているものの、テキストはそのまま読むことができると高谷は説明する。日本館は茶室を模して構想され、その四角い空間構造を確保するため入り口はあえて側面に移動されている。日本館を特徴づける、中央の開口部に取り付けられた方形のガラスからは外部の地上を見下ろすことができ、その深みを反射するハーフミラー・ガラスとあいまって「無」を強調する。このイメージには、数年前に京都の禅寺である大徳寺の真珠庵にある茶室にて、坂本とともに体験した突然の大雨がもたらした強烈な時間的、空間的経験も影響していると高谷は語る。アンビエントなインスタレーション作品は難解ながらも洗練されており、高度なテクノロジーを用いつつも自然と人間の内面に対する強い呼び起こしを伴う。それは、インスタグラムの撮影向きの、表面的な様相を持ち合わせてはいない。

初出:『il manifesto』紙(2022年4月22日、p.10)

JAPAN PAVILION

Dumb Type, geography questions us without hierarchies

Rossella Menegazzo

Dumb Type 2022. The name of the Japanese art collective, founded in Kyoto in 1984 by Takatani Shiro (1963) and Furuhashi Teiji (1960–1995), is enough to awaken nostalgia, emotions and enthusiasm in the many lovers of that avant-garde and experimental Japan who have already come to know the technological performances of Dumb Type in the 1980s and 1990s of the Bubble. Their name is itself expression of the desire to break forms and hierarchies. In fact not only do the members of the group change, increasing or decreasing in number depending on the project to be carried out, but their projects are the outcome of democratic creativity, of long nights spent discussing and proposing ideas freewheelingly that in the end find form in ever-changing installations and performances where the various artistic and scientific specializations merge.

IN THE PAVILION Japan 2022 one can experience the maturity achieved by the group, ten members of which are present on this occasion: Takatani Shiro and the famous musician and composer Sakamoto Ryuichi—who contributed with the musical base Playback recorded for the installation at the Haus der Kunst in Munich, which opens next May—, Furudate Ken, Hama Satoshi, Shiraki Ryo, Hara Marihiko, Tomari Hiromasa, Minami Takuya, Sora Norika and Takatani Yoko, as well as 16 other artists close to Sakamoto, authors of the environmental recordings made in different cities around the world, assembled in the soundtrack that for one hour takes the audience to a different dimension also thanks to the sounds created by the rotating vertical speakers that move the sound in the dark space of the Pavilion. A red laser light is projected on the walls alternating with beams and spots of white light and this creates a sort of horizon, developed on five lines, that rolls sometimes as a sign sometimes as a text. Short questions like the ones found in "Why is...?" books for children or school textbooks: "Where do volcanoes come from?," "How many oceans are there?," "What is a river?" raise universal questions about the origin of phenomena related to nature and geography. However, the interesting thing is to know that they are questions taken from an American geography book dating back to the 1850s when there was still little knowledge of the world and the universe compared to the opportunities of observation and analysis offered today by technology (just think of aerial photography and space missions which make it possible to have a complete view of the earth). Once the specific territorial reference is removed, which is American in this case, the questions seem to be always the same in any text of the world and make us ponder about the notion of country, border and our relationship with the world.

THE SCROLLING of the text alternates with the projection of images of moving clouds which, as Takatani points out, are understandable as such even though they are divided into pixels over five lines with a blurred effect like that of the reflection of landscape on water. The Pavilion was conceived as a tea room (chashitsu), so much so that, in order to maintain its square space, the entrance has been moved to the side, while the square glass in the middle of the room—which is typical of the Pavilion's architecture—overlooking the outside ground floor has been reinforced in its being "empty" (mu) through the use of mirror-covered walls that reflect its depth. As Takatani says- this image is evoked also by the intense experience of space and time he had a few years earlier with Sakamoto Ryuichi during a sudden downpour while they were in the tea room of the Shinjuan Zen temple of the Daitokuji complex in Kyoto. A rarefied and sophisticated environmental installation, which is high-tech but also has a strong reference to nature and interiority that does not lend itself to being hastily photographed and posted on Instagram.

il manifesto, April 22, 2022, p.10

PADIGLIONE GIAPPONE

Dumb Type, la geografia ci interroga senza gerarchie

Rossella Menegazzo

Dumb Type 2022. Basta il nome del collettivo artistico giapponese, fondato a Kyoto nel 1984 da Takatani Shiro (1963) e Furuhashi Teiji (1960–1995), a risvegliare nostalgie, emozioni ed entusiasmo nei tanti appassionati di quel Giappone d'avanguardia e sperimentale che già hanno conosciuto le performance tecnologiche dei Dumb Type negli anni ottanta e novanta della Bolla. Il loro nome esprime di per sé la voglia di rompere le forme e le gerarchie e infatti non solo i membri del gruppo cambiano, moltiplicandosi o riducendosi a seconda del progetto da realizzare, ma i loro progetti sono frutto di una creatività democratica, di lunghe notti spese discutendo e lanciando idee a ruota libera che alla fine trovano forma in installazioni e performance sempre diverse dove le varie specializzazioni artistiche e scientifiche si integrano.

NEL PADIGLIONE Giappone 2022 si sente la maturità raggiunta dal gruppo presente per l'occasione con dieci componenti: Takatani Shiro e il famoso musicista e compositore Sakamoto Ryuichi – che ha contribuito con la base Sonora Playback registrata per l'installazione alla Haus der Kunst di Monaco che inaugura il prossimo maggio –, Furudate Ken, Hama Satoshi, Shiraki Ryo, Hara Marihiko, Tomari Hiromasa, Minami Takuya, Sora Norika e Takatani Yoko, oltre ad altri 16 artisti vicini a Sakamoto, autori delle registrazioni ambientali realizzate in diverse città del mondo, montate nella traccia Sonora che per un'ora trasporta il pubblico in una dimensione diversa anche grazie alla sonorità creata dale casse verticali rotanti che muovono il suono nello spazio buio del Padiglione. Alle pareti è una proiezione di luce al laser rossa, alternata a fasci e spot di luce bianca, a creare una sorta di linea d'orizzonte sviluppata su cinque righe che scorre ora come segno ora come testo. Brevi frasi interrogative come quelle che si trovano nei libri «dei perché» per bambini o nei sussidiari di scuola: «Da dove nascono i vulcani?», «Quanti oceani ci sono?», «Cos'è un fiume?», sollevano quesiti universali sull'origine di fenomeni legati alla natura e alla geografia, ma la cosa interessante è sapere che sono frasi estrapolate da un testo di geografia americano degli anni cinquanta dell'Ottocento quando ancora del mondo e dell'universo vi era poca conoscenza rispetto alle possibilità di osservazione e analisi offerte oggi dalla tecnologia (si pensi solo alla fotografia aerea e alle missioni spaziali che permettono una visione totale del globo terrestre). Una volta tolto il riferimento specifico territoriale, americano in questo caso, le domande sembrano essere sempre le stesse in qualsiasi testo del mondo e fanno riflettere sulla nozione di Paese, di confine e sul nostro rapporto con il mondo.

LO SCORRIMENTO del testo alterna la proiezione di immagini di nuvole in movimento che, come sottolinea Takatani, rimangono leggibili come tali seppur divise in pixel su cinque righe con un effetto sfocato come quello che si ottiene dal riflesso di un paesaggio sull'acqua. Il Padiglione è stato concepito come una stanza per il tè (chashitsu) tanto che per mantenerne la spazialità quadrata l'entrata è stata spostata lateralmente, mentre il vetro quadrato al centro della stanza – caratteristico dell'architettura del Padiglione - che dà sul piano terra esterno è stato rinforzato nel suo essere «vuoto» (mu) attraverso l'uso di pareti a specchio che ne riverberano la profondità. Un'immagine evocata - dice Takatani - anche dall'esperienza intensa di spazio e tempo vissuta qualche anno prima con Sakamoto Ryuichi durante un improvviso scroscio di pioggia sceso mentre si trovavano nella stanza da tè del tempio zen Shinjuan del complesso Daitokuji a Kyoto. Un'installazione ambientale rarefatta e raffinata, ad alta tecnologia ma di forte richiamo alla natura e all'interiorità che non offre il fianco al mordi e fuggi dello scatto instagrammabile.

il manifesto, 22 aprile 2022, p.10

ダムタイプ

1984年結成。ヴィジュアル・アート、映像、コンピューター・プログラミング、音楽、ダンスなど、様々な分野の複数のアーティストによって構成されるグループ。プロジェクト毎に参加メンバーが変化して制作される作品は、既成のジャンルにとらわれない、あらゆる表現の形態を横断するマルチメディア・アートとして国内外の劇場やアートセンター、美術館等で紹介されてきた。特定のディレクターをおかずフラットでゆるやかなコラボレーションによる制作スタイルで、集団による共同制作の可能性を探る独自の活動を続けている。

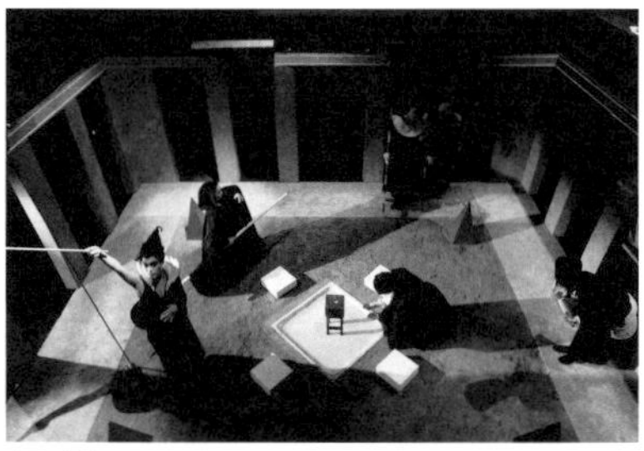

庭園の黄昏
Every Dog Has His Day

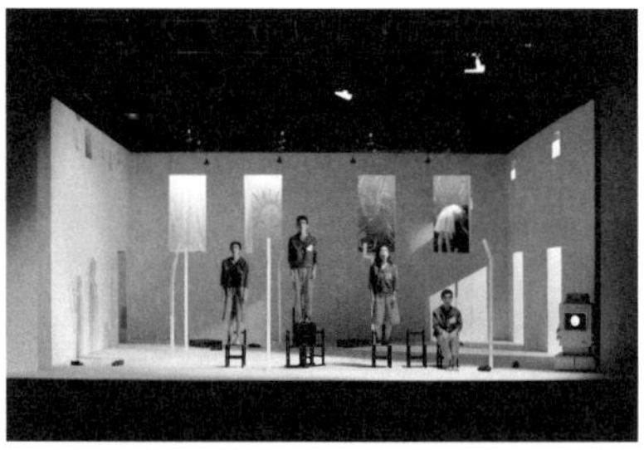

睡眠の計画 #5
Plan for Sleep #5

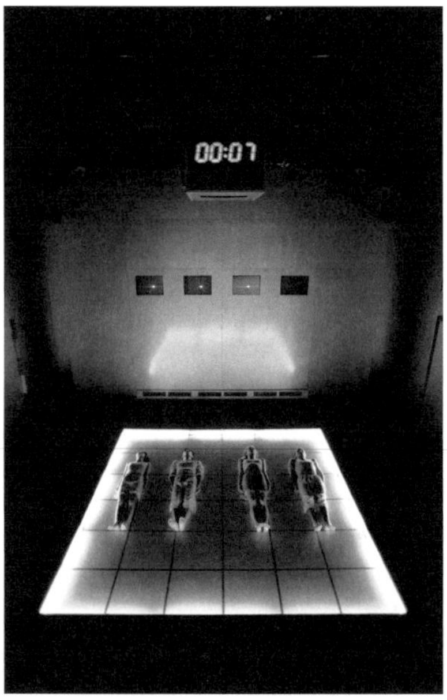

036-Pleasure Life

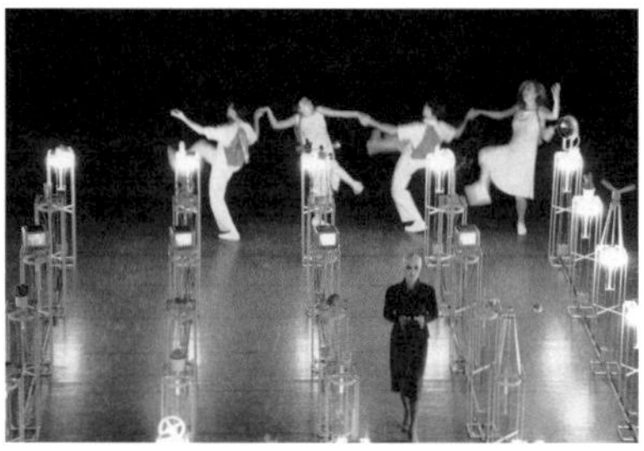

Pleasure Life

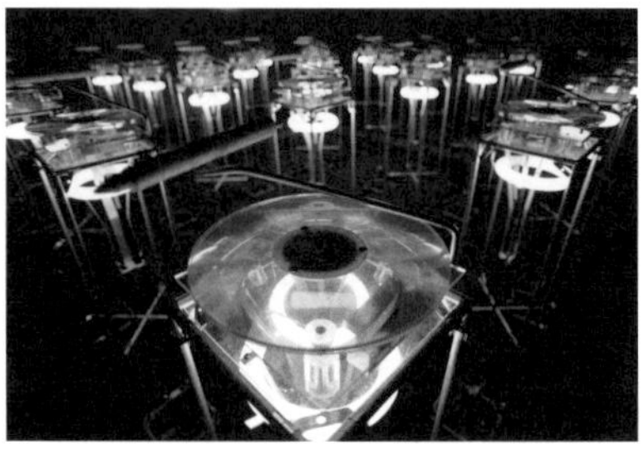

Playback

年譜1984–2022

1984年
京都にて結成
《賞賛すべき健康法》パフォーマンス｜京都市立芸術大学、京都
《ひとでのたし算》パフォーマンス｜京都市立芸術大学、京都
《睡眠の計画 #1》パフォーマンス｜京都市立芸術大学、京都
《睡眠の計画 #2》パフォーマンス｜アートスペース無門館、京都

1985年
《広場の秩序》インスタレーション、印刷物｜ギャラリー・ガーデンほか京都府内9か所
《風景収集狂者のための博物図鑑》パフォーマンス｜京都市立芸術大学、京都
《Listening Hour #1》パフォーマンス、インスタレーション、ビデオ｜ギャラリー・ガーデン、京都
《Listening Hour #2》パフォーマンス｜滋賀県立近代美術館、滋賀
《庭園の黄昏》パフォーマンス、カセットブック｜アートスペース無門館、京都

1986年
《睡眠の計画 #3》パフォーマンス｜オレンジルーム、大阪
《睡眠の計画 #8》インスタレーション、印刷物、シンポジウム｜梁画廊、京都
《睡眠の計画 #5》パフォーマンス｜「大阪国際演劇祭」、近鉄小劇場、大阪
《睡眠の計画》カセットブック

1987年
《Yes, the Salt of Passion—Part 6》パフォーマンス、インスタレーション｜ホテル・プロ・フォルマのキルステン・デールホルムとウィリー・フリント演出による、7月31日正午から8月1日正午まで24時間行われた作品のPART.6に参加｜「利賀国際演劇祭」、富山
《036-Pleasure Life》パフォーマンス、印刷物｜アートスペース無門館、京都
《サスペンスとロマンス》インスタレーション、コンサート｜つかしんホール、兵庫

1988年
《Pleasure Life》パフォーマンス｜原宿クエストホール、東京／「第1回ニューヨーク国際芸術祭」、P.S.122、ニューヨーク、USA／プンペンハウス劇場、ミュンスター、ドイツ／ICA、ロンドン、UK／国立美術館、コペンハーゲン、デンマーク／京都府立府民ホール・アルティ、京都
《The Nutcracker》パフォーマンス｜黒沢美香との共同制作｜青山円形劇場、東京

1989年
「Media Art Museum」NHK企画イベントの空間構成とアートディレクション｜原宿クエストホール、東京
《Playback》インスタレーション、ビデオ｜「アゲインスト・ネイチャー」展、USAおよび日本を巡回（1989年…サンフランシスコ近代美術館／アクロン美術館／MITリストヴィジュアルアートセンター、ボストン銀行アートギャラリー／1990年…シアトル美術館／シンシナティ現代美術センター／ニューヨーク大学グレイアートギャラリー／ヒューストン現代美術館／1991年…ICA名古屋、愛知）
《多角の旅 #1》パフォーマンス、ザ・ブリッジハウス・コレクションとの共同制作｜アートスペース無門館、京都

1990年
《多角の旅 #2》パフォーマンス、ザ・ブリッジハウス・コレクションとの共同制作｜ノーザンライトプラネタリウム、トロムソ、ノルウェー
《pH》パフォーマンス、インスタレーション、印刷物｜スパイラル、東京
《pH》パフォーマンス｜アートスペース無門館、京都

1991年
《pH》パフォーマンス｜京都市美術館、京都／ICA 名古屋、愛知／「グラナダ国際演劇フェスティバル」、青少年スタジアム、グラナダ、スペイン／「Art in the Anchorage」、クリエイティヴ・タイム、ニューヨーク、USA／モーダホール、大阪／チャプター、カーディフ、UK／トラムウェイ、グラスゴー、UK
《pH》ビデオ｜日本衛星放送［JSB］WOWOWとの共同制作

1992年 《pH》パフォーマンス｜「ウィーン芸術週間」、メッセパラス、ウィーン、オーストリア／
国立ソフィア王妃芸術センター、マドリード、スペイン／ブンペンハウス劇場、ミュンスター、ドイツ／
「ゾーンズ・オブ・ラヴ」展、シドニー現代美術館、シドニー、オーストラリア
「TV－Metropolis－Dumb Type－30'00"」スペイン国営放送制作・放映
《pH》ビデオ｜黄金の太陽賞（TTVV-Riccione、イタリア）受賞／ベスト・ステージ・レコーディング賞
（IMZ Dance Screen 92、ドイツ）受賞
《S/N #1》インスタレーション｜「バイナリー・エラ」展、イクセル美術館、ブリュッセル、ベルギー
（1993年…クンストハーレ、ウィーン、オーストリアへ巡回）
《Enigma of the Late Afternoon》パフォーマンス｜ホテル・プロ・フォルマとの共同制作｜
ニイ・カールスベルグ・グリプトテク美術館、コペンハーゲン、デンマーク
《S/N #2》インスターション｜「アナザーワールド」展、水戸芸術館、茨城

1993年 《pH》パフォーマンス｜スパイラルホール、東京／
「6月祭」、シアターハウス・ゲスナーアレー、チューリッヒ、スイス
《S/Nの為のセミナー・ショー》パフォーマンス&トーク｜
アートスペース無門館、京都／藤沢市湘南台文化センター市民シアター、神奈川
《pH》ビデオ｜「ビデオ・フィルム・ダンス・フェスティバル」、リュブリャナ、スロヴェニア
《S/N #1》インスタレーション｜「第5回ふくい国際ビデオ・ビエンナーレ」、福井県立美術館、福井

1994年 《LOVE/SEX/DEATH/MONEY/LIFE》インスタレーション｜「人間の条件」展、スパイラル、東京
《S/N #1》インスタレーション｜「戦後日本の前衛美術」展、横浜美術館、神奈川／
グッゲンハイム・ソーホー、ニューヨーク、USA（1995年…サンフランシスコ近代美術館
Center for the Arts at Yerba Buena Gardens、サンフランシスコ、USAへ巡回）
《S/N》パフォーマンス｜「アデレード・フェスティバル」、アデレード、オーストラリア／
モントリオール現代美術館、モントリオール、カナダ／オン・ザ・ボーズ、キング・パフォーマンス・
シアター、シアトル、USA／「第1回神奈川芸術フェスティバル」、ランドマークホール、神奈川
《pH》ビデオ｜「ビデオ・フィルム・ダンス・フェスティバル」、香港

1995年 《S/N》パフォーマンス｜スパイラルホール、東京／「VISAS国際フェスティバル」、ル・マネージュ
国立舞台、ラ・ルナ、モブージュ、フランス／「ヨーロッパ文化首都 ルクセンブルグ95」、
エッシュ劇場、ルクセンブルク／Cankarjev Dom、リュブリャナ、スロヴェニア／ブンペンハウス劇場、
ミュンスターランドホール、ミュンスター、ドイツ／「EXITフェスティバル」、クレテイユ芸術館、
クレテイユ、フランス／「Kunsten Festival Des Arts」、ブリュッセル、ベルギー／「チューリッヒ・
シアター・スペクタクル」、ヴェルフト劇場、チューリッヒ、スイス／「オーフス・フェスティバル」、
ミュージックヒュッセ、オーフス、デンマーク／「SPIEL.ART」、ムッファターレ、ミュンヘン、ドイツ／
「国際舞台芸術祭」、カストロ・アルヴェス劇場、サルバドール、ブラジル／「国際舞台芸術祭」、
SESCアンシエタ、サンパウロ、ブラジル
《S/N》CD｜NEWSIC、スパイラル、ワコールアートセンター、東京
《S/N》パフォーマンス｜第2回読売演劇大賞・選考委員特別賞受賞
《pH》パフォーマンス｜「VISAS国際フェスティバル」、ル・マネージュ国立舞台、ラ・ルナ、モブージュ、
フランス／「EXITフェスティバル」、クレテイユ芸術館、クレテイユ、フランス／「Today's Japan」、
ハーバーフロント・センター、トロント、カナダ
《LOVE/SEX/DEATH/MONEY/LIFE》インスタレーション｜「Fluctuations Fugitives」展、
イヴォナムール・パリ画廊、パリ、フランス
《S/N インターネット・ヴァージョン》インターネット・プロジェクト｜NTT インターコミュニケーション'95
「on the Web ―ネットワークの中のミュージアム―」

1996年 《S/N》パフォーマンス｜「TOKYO演劇フェア '96」、東京芸術劇場、東京／京都府立府民ホール・
アルティ、京都／「香港芸術節」、香港文化センター、香港／「ニュージーランド国際芸術祭」、Shed 1、
ウェリントン、ニュージーランド／テアトロ・セントラル、セビリア、スペイン／「EXITフェスティバル」、
クレテイユ芸術館、クレテイユ、フランス
《Monkey Business Class》パフォーマンス｜ホテル・プロ・フォルマ、エリザベス・ディラー＋
リカルド・スコフィディオおよびウィリー・フリントとの共同制作｜マルメ・ミュージックシアター、
マルメ、スウェーデン／Albertslund Music Theatre、コペンハーゲン、デンマーク

1997年 《OR》パフォーマンス｜「VIAフェスティバル」、ル・マネージュ国立舞台、マネージュ劇場、
モブージュ、フランス／「EXITフェスティバル」、クレテイユ芸術館、クレテイユ、フランス／「アルス・
エレクトロニカ・フェスティバル1997」、デザイン・センター、リンツ、オーストリア／パークタワー
ホール、東京／「フェスティバル・ドートンヌ・パリ」、クレテイユ芸術館、クレテイユ、フランス
《OR》インスタレーション｜NTTインターコミュニケーション・センター［ICC］
（常設展示2000年9月まで）、東京
《OR》コンサート｜「Palermo di Scena」、サンタ・マリア・デッロ・スパシモ、パレルモ、イタリア／
神戸アートビレッジセンター、兵庫／スパイラルホール、東京

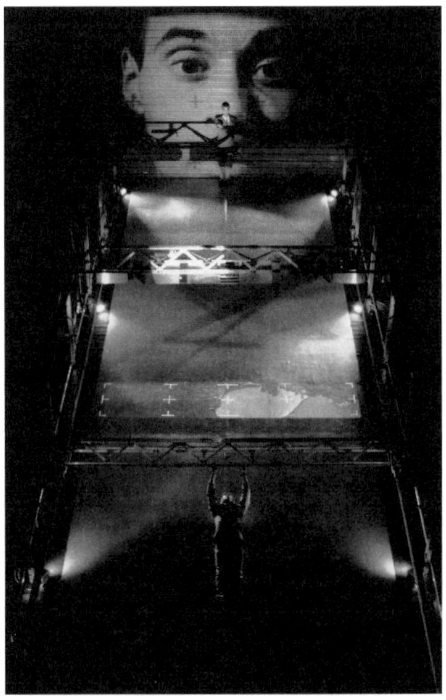
pH

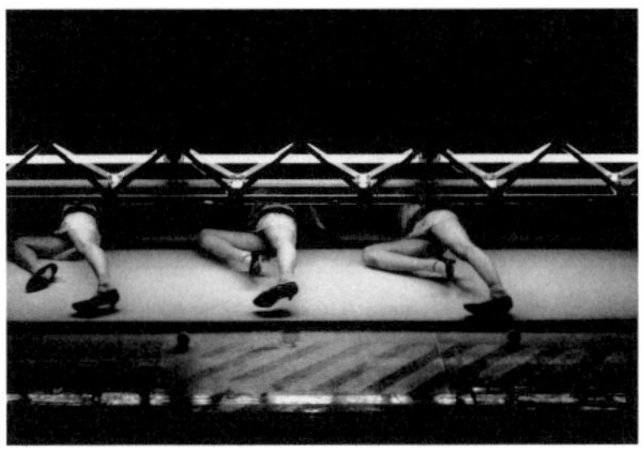
pH

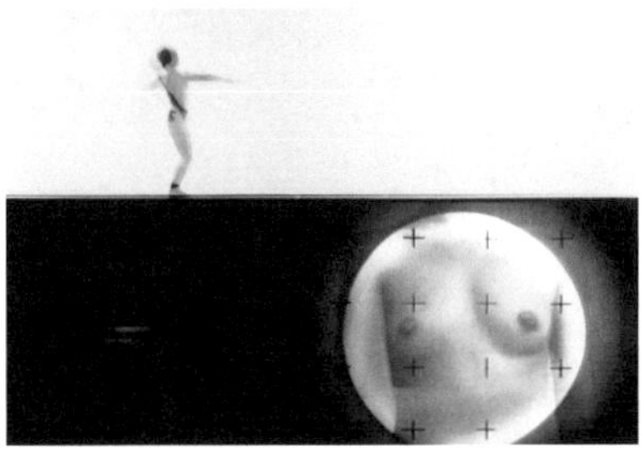
S/N

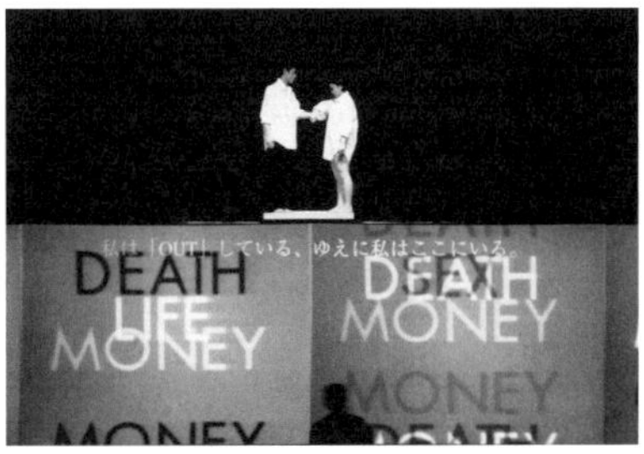

S/N

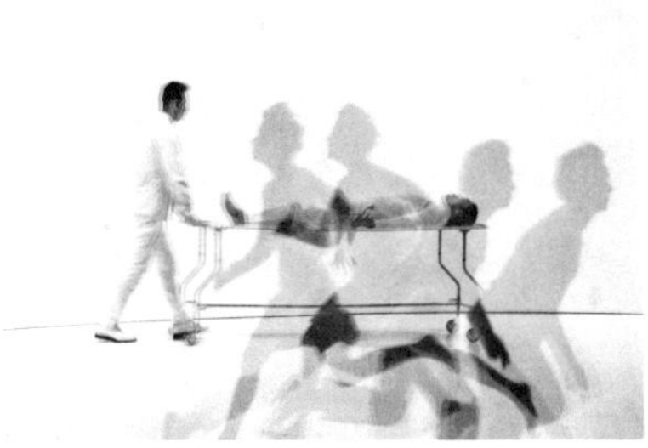
OR

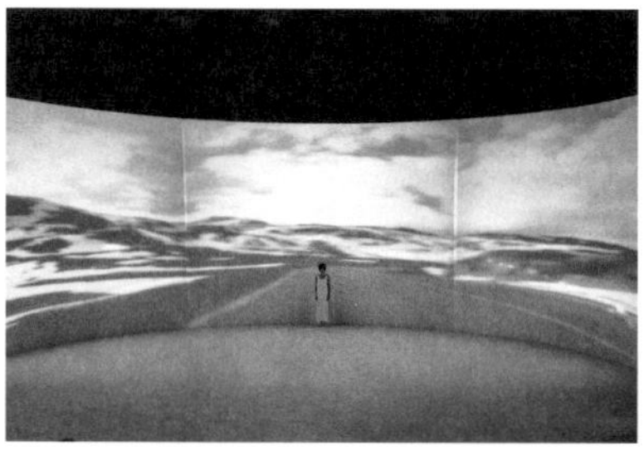

OR

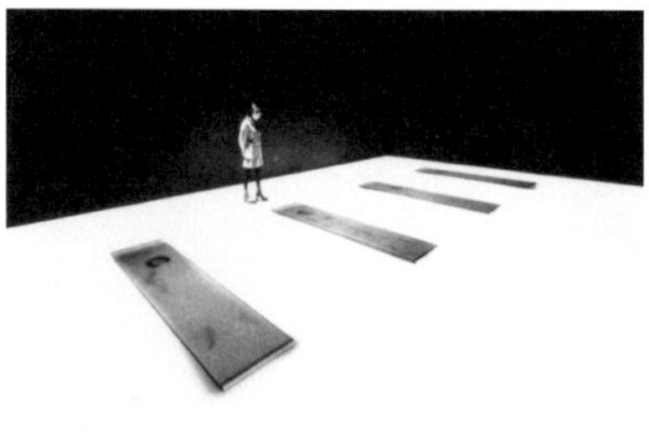

OR installation

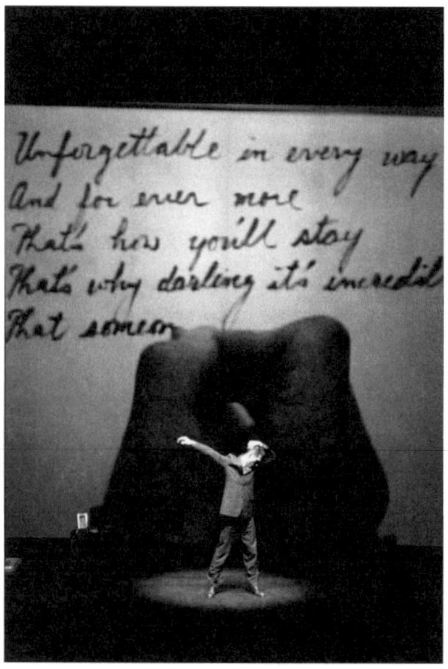

memorandum

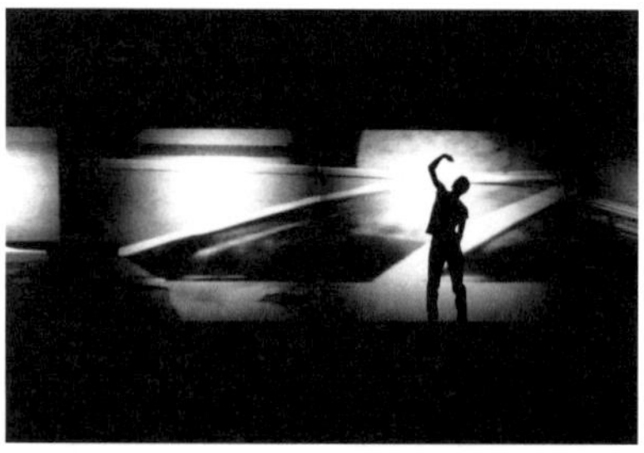

memorandum

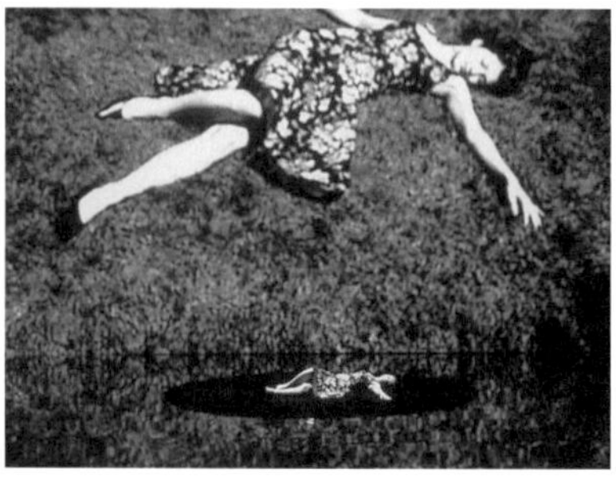

Voyage

1998年　《Dangerous Visions》コンサート｜Art Zoyd、リール国立管弦楽団との共同制作｜リール、モブージュ、クレテイユ（フランス）で上演
《S/N #1》インスタレーション｜ヴォイス・ギャラリー、京都
《OR》パフォーマンス｜「Julidans」、市立劇場、アムステルダム、オランダ／「EXPO '98 LISBOA」、ベレム文化センター、リスボン、ポルトガル／「チューリッヒ・シアター・スペクタクル」、ヴェルフト劇場、チューリッヒ、スイス／「het pact」、de warande stad turnhout、トゥルンホウト、ベルギー／「BITE 98」、バービカン・センター、ロンドン、UK／カンプナーゲル劇場、ハンブルク、ドイツ／Dansens Hus、ストックホルム、スウェーデン
《LOVE/SEX/DEATH/MONEY/LIFE》インスタレーション｜「どないやねん　現代日本の創造力」展、École nationale supérieure des beaux-arts、パリ、フランス

1999年　《Sweet Memories》（仮題）パフォーマンス、公開リハーサル｜「スタジオ・ビデオ・ダンス・フェスティバル」、カリステ劇場、アジャクシオ、コルシカ、フランス
《OR》パフォーマンス｜高知県立美術館ホール、高知／「芸術祭典・京 '99」、京都市北文化会館、京都／「ドナウ・フェスティバル」、Theaterhaus Alte Sporthalle、クレムス、オーストリア／オン・ザ・ボーズ、シアトル、USA／PICA（ポートランド現代美術協会）、ポートランド、USA／ウォーカー・アート・センター、ミネアポリス、USA／シカゴ現代美術館、シカゴ、USA
《LOVE/SEX/DEATH/MONEY/LIFE》インスタレーション｜「ファンシーダンス」展、アートソンジェ美術館、慶州、大韓民国／アートソンジェ・センター、ソウル、大韓民国
《memorandum》パフォーマンス｜「Festival de danse」、ル・マネージュ国立舞台、モブージュ、フランス／「フェスティバル・ドートンヌ・パリ」、クレテイユ芸術館、クレテイユ、フランス／世界文化館、ベルリン、ドイツ／「Festival de Otoño」YSARCA、アルベニス劇場、マドリード、スペイン

2000年　《OR》インスタレーション｜「Musiques en Scène」展、リヨン現代美術館（収蔵）、リヨン、フランス／「Gendai: 日本の現代美術―身体と空間の間」展、ワルシャワ現代アートセンター、ワルシャワ、ポーランド
《memorandum》パフォーマンス｜「シャルルロワ・ダンス」、シャルルロワ、ベルギー／GRAME＋メゾン・ド・ラ・ダンス、リヨン、フランス／CDC（トゥールーズ振付センター）＋TNT（トゥールーズ国立劇場）、トゥールーズ、フランス／テアトロ・セントラル、セビリア、スペイン／「Julidans」、市立劇場、アムステルダム、オランダ／「日本のダンス：国際サマーフェスティバル」、タンツハウスNRW、デュッセルドルフ、ドイツ／「La Bâtie Festival de Genève」、ジュネーヴ、スイス／高知県立美術館ホール、高知／新国立劇場、東京／シアター・ドラマシティ、大阪
《cascade》インスタレーション＆パフォーマンス｜「Stanze e Segreti」展、サローネ・デル・モービレ、ミラノ、イタリア
《LOVE/SEX/DEATH/MONEY/LIFE》インスタレーション｜「vision.ruhr」展、オストワル美術館、ドルトムント、ドイツ

2001年　《cascade》インスタレーション＆パフォーマンス｜「Translated Acts: Performance and Body Art from East Asia」展、世界文化館、ベルリン、ドイツ

2002年　《memorandum》パフォーマンス｜テルアビブ新オペラ劇場、テルアビブ、イスラエル／シカゴ現代美術館、シカゴ、USA／オン・ザ・ボーズ、シアトル、USA／PICA（ポートランド現代美術協会）、ニューマーク劇場、ポートランド、USA／ウォーカー・アート・センター、ミネアポリス、USA／「アート・ロック・フェスティバル」、La Passerelle、サン・ブリュ、フランス／クレテイユ芸術館、クレテイユ、フランス／「シンガポール芸術祭」、ヴィクトリア劇場、シンガポール／国際交流基金クアラルンプール日本文化センター、イスタナ・ブダヤ国立劇場、クアラルンプール、マレーシア
《OR》インスタレーション｜トゥールーズ高等美術学校、トゥールーズ、フランス
《Voyage》パフォーマンス｜CDC（トゥールーズ振付センター）＋TNT（トゥールーズ国立劇場）、トゥールーズ、フランス／ル・パルヴィス国立舞台、イボス＝タルブ、フランス／彩の国さいたま芸術劇場、埼玉／シアター・ドラマシティ、大阪／国立オペラ＆バレエ劇場、ヴィリニュス、リトアニア／ヴァネムイネ劇場、タルトゥ、エストニア／国立オペラ劇場、リガ、ラトビア／Le-Maillon Théâtre de Strasbourg、ストラスブール、フランス
《Voyages》インスタレーション｜NTTインターコミュニケーション・センター［ICC］、東京

2003年　《Voyage》パフォーマンス｜Deutsches Nationaltheater und Staatskapelle Weimar、ワイマール、ドイツ／滋賀県立芸術劇場びわ湖ホール、滋賀／REDCAT（Roy and Edna Disney/CalArts Theater）、ロサンゼルス、USA／クレテイユ芸術館、クレテイユ、フランス
《memorandum》パフォーマンス｜「国際モダンダンス・フェスティバル」、KCAF芸術劇場、ソウル、大韓民国／「ヴェネチア・ビエンナーレ国際コンテンポラリーダンス・フェスティバル」、アルセナーレ小劇場、ヴェネチア、イタリア／バンコク・プレイハウス、バンコク、タイ／「メルボルン国際芸術フェスティバル」、フォーラム・シアター、メルボルン、オーストラリア／REDCAT（Roy and Edna Disney/CalArts Theater）、ロサンゼルス、USA／ピッツバーグ・ダンス・カウンシル、ピッツバーグ、USA
《OR》インスタレーション｜「CINÉMAS DU FUTUR」展、LILLE 2004 ヨーロッパ文化首都 Euralille、リール、フランス

2004年　《Voyages》インスタレーション｜山口情報芸術センター［YCAM］、山口
《Voyage》パフォーマンス｜山口情報芸術センター［YCAM］、山口／Novel Hall for Performing Arts、台北、台湾／「Tanztheater 3 wochen mit Pina Bausch」、Schauspielhaus、デュッセルドルフ、ドイツ

2005年　《Voyage》パフォーマンス｜アングレーム劇場、アングレーム、フランス／Le Carré des Jalles、サン＝メダール＝アン＝ジャル、フランス／Dansens Hus、ストックホルム、スウェーデン／「ベルゲン国際フェスティバル」、ベルゲン、ノルウェー／「国際モダンダンス・フェスティバル」、KCAF芸術劇場、ソウル、大韓民国／Muffathalle、ミュンヘン、ドイツ／Altstadherbst Kulturfestival Düsseldorf、デュッセルドルフ、ドイツ
《OR》インスタレーション｜TESLA BERLIN、ベルリン、ドイツ

2006年　《Voyage》パフォーマンス｜La Comète—Scène Nationale de Châlons-en-Champagne、シャロン＝アン＝シャンパーニュ、フランス／ニーム劇場、ニーム、フランス／Posthof、リンツ、オーストリア／トラムウェイ、グラスゴー、UK／「エクソダス・フェスティバル」、Cankarjev Dom、リュブリャナ、スロヴェニア／「メルボルン国際芸術フェスティバル」、プレイハウス劇場、メルボルン、オーストラリア

2007年　《Voyages》インスタレーション｜「身体・媒体」展、上海市彫刻芸術センター、0 ART CENTER、復旦大学上海視覚芸術学院、上海、中華人民共和国／「NAMURA ART MEETING '04–'34」、名村造船所跡地スタジオ・パルティッタ、大阪／「Vom Funken zum Pixel」展、マルティン・グロピウス・バウ、ベルリン、ドイツ

2008年　《Voyage》パフォーマンス｜「XI FESTIVAL IBEROAMERICANO DE TEATRO DE BOGOTA」、ボゴタ、コロンビア／EMPAC (Experimental Media & Performing Arts Center)、レンセラー工科大学、ニューヨーク州トロイ、USA／モントクレア州立大学、アレキサンダー・カッサー劇場、ニュージャージー州モントクレア、USA／LA FILATURE劇場、ミュルーズ、フランス／ル・ヴォルカン国立舞台、ル・アーブル、フランス
《S/N》パフォーマンス記録映像上映｜「NTTインターコミュニケーション・センター［ICC］」、東京

2009年　《Voyage》パフォーマンス｜O.M.M.A. (Organismos Megarou Mousikis Athinon)、アテネ・コンサートホール、アテネ、ギリシャ共和国／SEMEC (Societe d'Economie Mixte pour les Evenements Cannois)、Palais des Festivals et des Congrès、ドビュッシー劇場、カンヌ、フランス
《OR》《memorandum》DVD｜コモンズ、東京

2010年　《S/N》パフォーマンス記録映像上映｜「六本木クロッシング2010展：芸術は可能か?」展、森美術館、東京
《pH》《S/N》《OR》《memorandum》《Voyage》パフォーマンス記録映像上映｜NTTインターコミュニケーション・センター［ICC］、東京
《LOVE/SEX/DEATH/MONEY/LIFE》インスタレーション｜「LIFE with ART―受けとめ、そして、渡す人―」展、京都精華大学ギャラリーフロール、京都

2012年　《pH》ビデオ｜「Double Vision: contemporary art from Japan」展、モスクワ近代美術館、モスクワ、ロシア

2013年　《pH》《S/N》《OR》パフォーマンス記録映像上映｜「Re: Quest—1970年代以降の日本現代美術」展、ソウル大学美術館、ソウル、大韓民国

2014年　《MEMORANDUM OR VOYAGE》インスタレーション｜「新たな系譜学を求めて――跳躍／痕跡／身体」展、東京都現代美術館、東京
《memorandum》パフォーマンス記録映像上映｜「Code Act」展、コリアナ美術館 Space*C、ソウル、大韓民国

2017年　《MEMORANDUM OR VOYAGE》インスタレーション｜「Reenacting History: Collective Actions and Everyday Gestures」展、MMCA国立現代美術館 果川館、果川、大韓民国／「ROMAEUROPA DIGITALIFE」展、エスポジツィオーニ宮殿、ローマ、イタリア
《MEMORANDUM OR VOYAGE》インスタレーション｜ポンピドゥー・センター、フランス（収蔵）

2018年　個展「**ダムタイプ｜アクション＋リフレクション**」｜ポンピドゥー・センター・メッス、フランス
《pH》《S/N》パフォーマンス記録映像 特別上映｜「YCC Temporary」、YCCヨコハマ創造都市センター、神奈川

2019年　《**DUMB TYPE 新作プロジェクト――ワーク・イン・プログレス**》パフォーマンス、公開リハーサル｜ロームシアター京都、京都
個展「**ダムタイプ｜アクション＋リフレクション**」｜東京都現代美術館、東京

2020年　《2020》パフォーマンス｜ロームシアター京都、京都［新型コロナウイルス感染症のため公演中止］
《2020》パフォーマンス記録映像上映｜ロームシアター京都、京都

2022年　《2022》インスタレーション｜第59回ヴェネチア・ビエンナーレ国際美術展 日本館、ヴェネチア、イタリア
個展「**ダムタイプ**」、Haus der Kunst、ミュンヘン、ドイツ

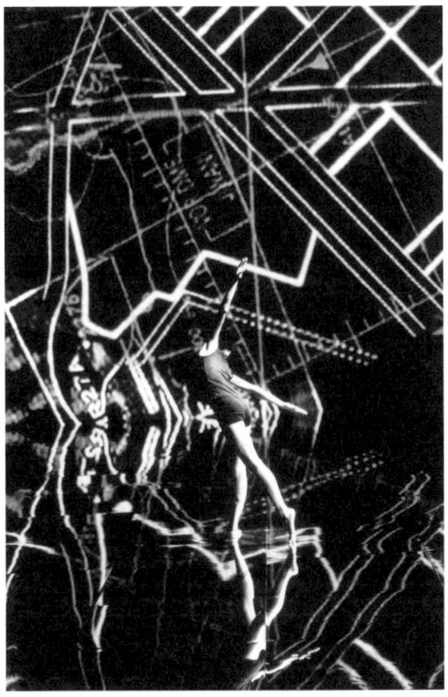

Voyage

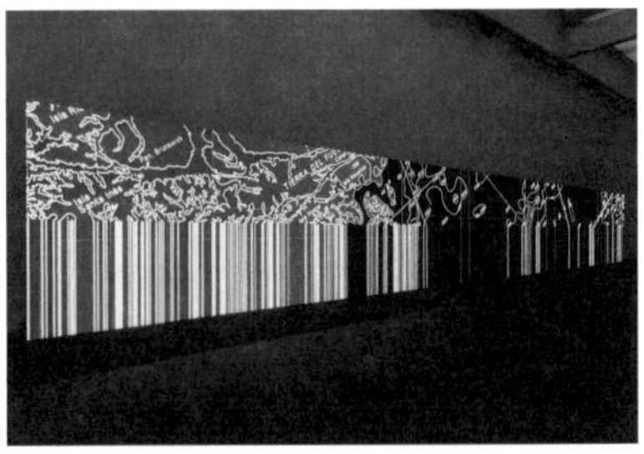

MEMORANDUM OR VOYAGE

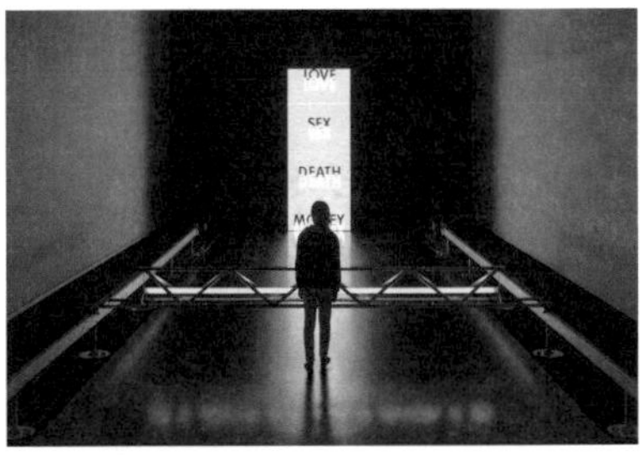

pH（手前｜front）| LOVE/SEX/DEATH/MONEY/LIFE（奥｜back）

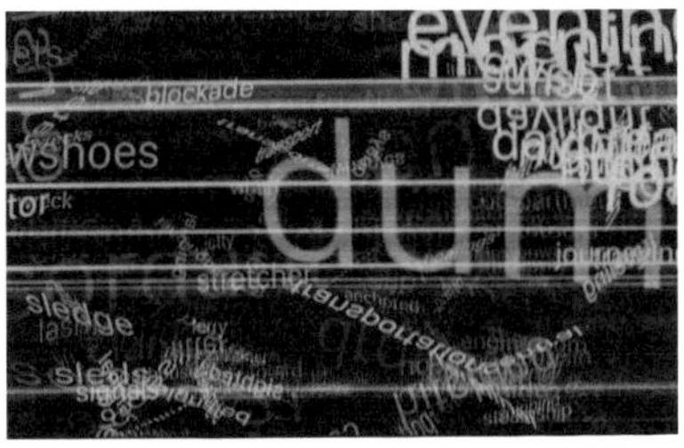

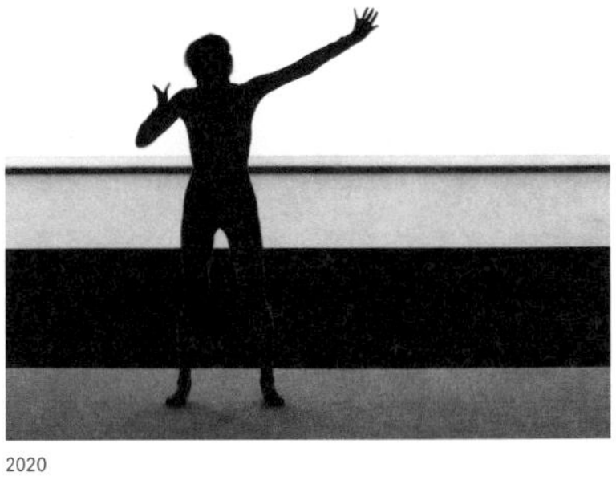

2020

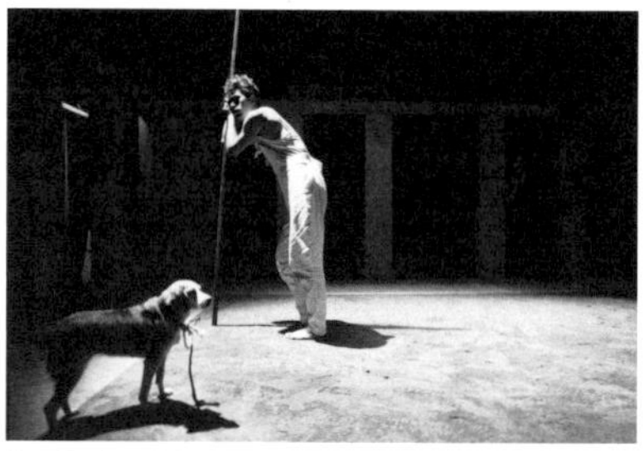

Every Dog Has His Day
庭園の黄昏

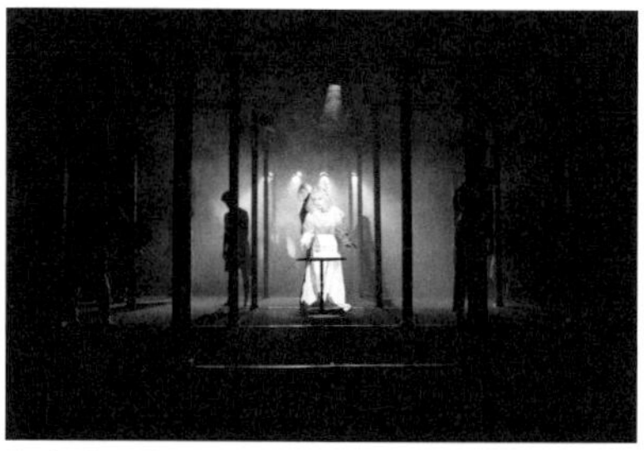

Plan for Sleep #3
睡眠の計画 #3

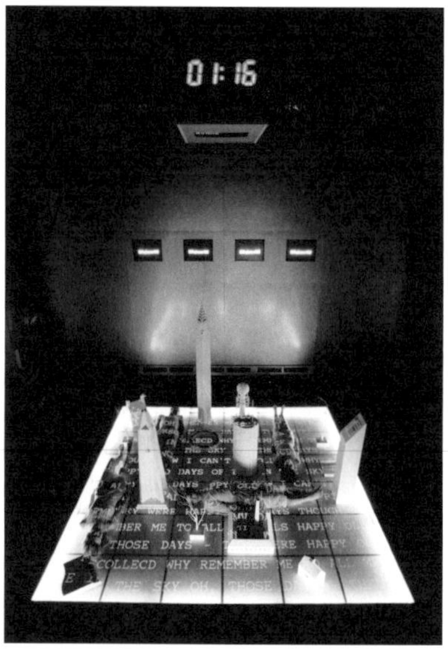

036-Pleasure Life

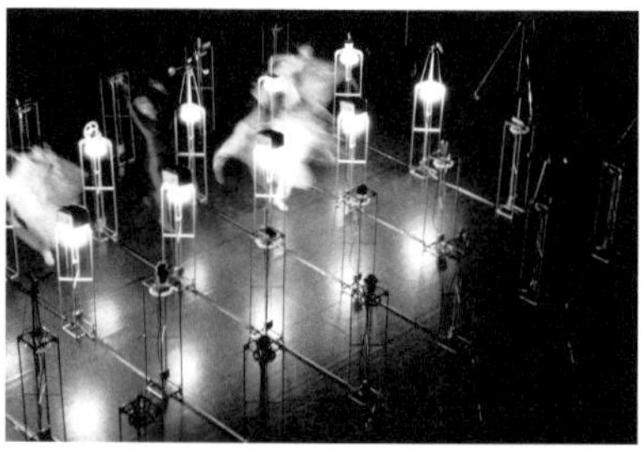

Pleasure Life

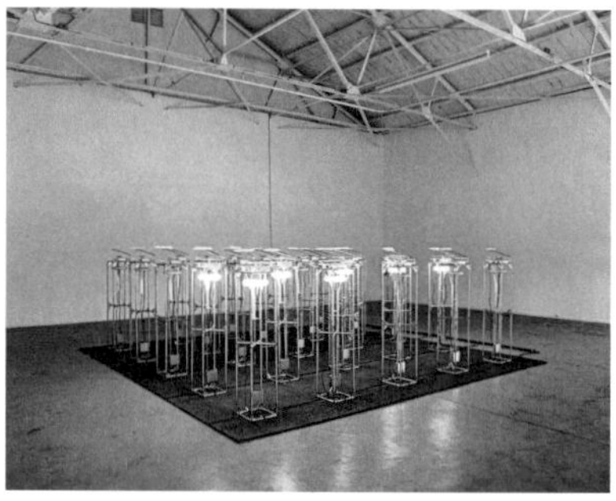

Playback

DUMB TYPE

Founded in 1984, Dumb Type is comprised of artists from diverse backgrounds—visual art, music, video, dance, design, programming and other fields—all contributing to a great variety of stage and installation productions over the years. They have maintained an open-ended creative style with no fixed director and a changing roster of members participating in each new production as part of their on-going exploration of ever new possibilities in artistic collaboration. Since its formation, Dumb Type has worked toward a broadening of the possibilities for artistic expression. Derived from the diversity of its members and from the different media the group uses, Dumb Type's work ranges across such diverse media as art exhibitions, performances and live music concerts. Their interdisciplinary efforts continue to transcend existing genres of fine art, theater and dance. Regardless of genre, the essence of their work addresses a variety of social issues related to contemporary society, and the today's technological reality on a global scale.

Chronicle 1984–2022

1984
founded in Kyoto, Japan
The Admirable Health Method | performance | Kyoto City University of Arts, Kyoto, Japan
An Asteroid Addition | performance | Kyoto City University of Arts, Kyoto, Japan
Plan for Sleep #1 | performance | Kyoto City University of Arts, Kyoto, Japan
Plan for Sleep #2 | performance | Artspace Mumonkan, Kyoto, Japan

1985
The Order of the Square | installation, printed matter | Gallery Garden and 9 other locations, Kyoto, Japan
An Encyclopedia for Landscapemaniacs | performance | Kyoto City University of Arts, Kyoto, Japan
Listening Hour #1 | performance, installation | Gallery Garden, Kyoto, Japan
Listening Hour #2 | performance | The Museum of Modern Art, Shiga, Japan
Every Dog Has His Day | performance, cassette-book | Artspace Mumonkan, Kyoto, Japan

1986
Plan for Sleep #3 | performance | Orange Room, Osaka, Japan
Plan for Sleep #8 | installation, printed matter, symposium | Ryo Gallery, Kyoto, Japan
Plan for Sleep #5 | performance | "Osaka International Arts Festival," Osaka, Japan
Plan for Sleep | cassette-book

1987
Yes, the Salt of Passion - Part 6 | performance, installation | collaboration with Hotel Pro Forma and Willie Flindt | "Toga International Arts Festival," Toyama, Japan
036-Pleasure Life | performance, printed matter | Artspace Mumonkan, Kyoto, Japan
Suspense and Romance | installation, music concert | Tsukashin Hall, Hyogo, Japan

1988
Pleasure Life | performance | Quest Hall, Tokyo, Japan / "The 1st New York International Festival of The Arts," Performance Space 122, New York, USA / Theater im Pumpenhaus, Münster, Germany / ICA, London, UK / Statens Museum for Kunst, Copenhagen, Denmark / ALTI, Kyoto, Japan
The Nutcracker | performance | collaboration with Mika Kurosawa | Aoyama Enkei Theatre, Tokyo, Japan

1989
"Media Art Museum" | art direction for the event presented by NHK | Quest Hall, Tokyo, Japan
Playback | installation, video | in the exhibition "Against Nature," San Francisco Museum of Modern Art, USA / Akron Art Museum, USA / MIT List Visual Arts Center, Bank of Boston Art Gallery, USA
In 1990 - Seattle Art Museum, USA / The Contemporary Arts Center, Cincinnati, USA / Grey Art Gallery, New York University, USA / Contemporary Arts Museum, Houston, USA
In 1991 - ICA, Nagoya, Aichi, Japan
The Polygonal Journey #1 | performance | collaboration with The Bridgehouse Collection | Artspace Mumonkan, Kyoto, Japan

1990
The Polygonal Journey #2 | performance | collaboration with The Bridgehouse Collection | Northern Light Planetarium, Tromsø, Norway
pH | performance, installation, printed matter | Spiral, Tokyo, Japan
pH | performance | Artspace Mumonkan, Kyoto, Japan

1991
pH | performance | Kyoto Municipal Museum of the Arts, Kyoto, Japan / ICA Nagoya, Aichi, Japan / "Festival Internacional de Teatro de Granada," Estadio de la Juventud, Granada, Spain / "Art in the Anchorage," Creative Time, New York, USA / Moda Hall, Osaka, Japan / Chapter, Cardiff, UK / Tramway, Glasgow, UK
pH | video | co-produced with Japan Satellite Broadcasting WOWOW, Japan

1992 **pH** | performance | "Wiener Festwochen," Messepalast, Vienna, Austria / Centro de Arte Reina Sofia, Madrid, Spain / Theater im Pumpenhaus, Münster, Germany / "Zones of Love," Museum of Contemporary Art, Sydney, Australia

TV - METROPOLIS - DUMB TYPE - 30'00" | produced and broadcasted by Televisión Española, Spain

pH | video | Sole d'Oro Award (TTVV-Riccione, ITALY) / Best Stage Recording, Studio Adaptation Award (IMZ Dance Screen 92, Germany)

S/N #1 | installation | in the exhibition "The Binary Era," Museurn of Ixelles, Bruxelles, Belgium
In 1993 - Kunsthalle, Vienna, Austria

Enigma of the Late Afternoon | performance | collaboration with Hotel Pro Forma | Ny Carlsberg Glyptotek Museum, Copenhagen, Denmark

S/N #2 | installation | in the exhibition "Another World," ATM Contemporary Art Gallery, Ibaraki, Japan

1993 **pH** | performance | Spiral Hall, Tokyo, Japan / "Junefestival," Theaterhaus Gessnerallee, Zürich, Switzerland

Seminar Show for *S/N* | performance & talk | Artspace Mumonkan, Kyoto, Japan / Shonandai Culture Center Civic Theater, Kanagawa, Japan

pH | video | "Video Film Dance Festival," Ljubljana, Slovenia

S/N #1 | installation | "The 5th Fukui International Video Biennale," Fukui Fine Arts Museum, Fukui, Japan

1994 **LOVE/SEX/DEATH/MONEY/LIFE** | installation | in the exhibition "Of the Human Condition: Hope and Despair at the End of the Century," Spiral, Tokyo, Japan

S/N #1 | installation | in the exhibition "Japanese Art After 1945 Scream Against the Sky," Yokohama Art Museum, Yokohama, Japan / Guggenheim SOHO, New York, USA
In 1995 - San Francisco Museum of Modern Art, Center for the Arts at Yerba Buena Gardens, San Francisco, USA

S/N | performance | "Adelaide Festival," Adelaide, Australia / Musée d'Art Contemporain de Montréal, Montréal, Canada / On The Boards, The King Performance Theater, Seattle, USA / "Kanagawa Arts Festival," Landmark Hall, Kanagawa, Japan

pH | video | "Video Film Dance Festival," Hong Kong

1995 **S/N** | performance | Spiral Hall, Tokyo, Japan / "VISAS Festival International," Le Manège Scène Nationale, La Luna, Maubeuge, France / "Luxembourg 95: Ville Européenne de la Culture," Théâtre d'Esch, Luxembourg / Cankarjev Dom, Ljubljana, Slovenia / Theater im Pumpenhaus, Halle Münsterland, Münster, Germany / "EXIT Festival," Maison des Arts de Créteil, Créteil, France / "Kunsten Festival des Arts," Théâtre Varia, Bruxelles, Belgium / "Züricher Theater Spektakel," Theater Werft, Zürich, Switzerland / "Aarhus Festuge," Musikhuset, Aarhus, Denmark / "SPIEL.ART," Muffathalle, München, Germany / "Festival Internacional de Artes Cênicas," Teatro Castro Alves, Salvador, Brazil / "Festival Internacional de Artes Cênicas," Sesc Anchieta, São Paulo, Brazil

S/N | CD | released by NEWSIC, Spiral, Wacoal Art Center, Tokyo, Japan

pH | performance | "VISAS Festival International," Le Manège Scène Nationale, La Luna, Maubeuge, France / "EXIT Festival," Maison des Arts de Créteil, Créteil, France / "Today's Japan," Harbourfront Centre, Toronto, Canada

LOVE/SEX/DEATH/MONEY/LIFE | installation | in the exhibition "Fluctuations Fugitives," Espace d'Art Yvonamor Palix, Paris, France

S/N internet version | internet project | NTT InterCommunication '95 "on the Web—The Museum Inside The Network"

1996 **S/N** | performance | "Tokyo Theater Fair 96," Tokyo Geijutsu Gekijo, Tokyo, Japan / ALTI, Kyoto, Japan / "Hong Kong Arts Festival," Hong Kong Culture Centre Studio Theatre, Hong Kong / "New Zealand International Festival of the Arts," Shed 1, Wellington, New Zealand / Teatro Central, Sevilla, Spain / "EXIT Festival," Maison des Arts de Créteil, Créteil, France

Monkey Business Class | performance | collaboration with Hotel Pro Forma, Elizabeth Diller + Ricardo Scofidio, and Willie Flindt | Malmö Musikteater Storan, Malmö, Sweden / Albertslund Music Theatre, Copenhagen, Denmark

1997 **OR** | performance | "Festival VIA," Le Manège Scène Nationale, Théâtre du Manège, Maubeuge, France / "EXIT Festival," Maison des Arts de Créteil, Créteil, France / "Ars Electronica 1997 Fleshfactor," Design Centre, Linz, Austria / Park Tower Hall, Tokyo, Japan / "Festival d'Automne à Paris," Maison des Arts de Créteil, Créteil, France

OR | installation | NTT InterCommunication Center [ICC] (permanent exhibition until September 2000), Tokyo, Japan

OR | concert | "Palermo di Scena," Santa Maria dello Spasimo, Palermo, Italy / Kobe Art Village Center, Hyogo, Japan / Spiral Hall, Tokyo, Japan

1998 **Dangerous Visions** | concert | collaboration with Art Zoyd and Lille National Orchestra | toured in Lille, Maubeuge and Creteil, France

S/N #1 | installation | Voice Gallery, Kyoto, Japan

OR | performance | "Julidans," Stadsschouwburg, Amsterdam, The Netherlands / "EXPO '98 Lisboa: Mergulho no future festival," Centro Cultural de Belém, Lisbon, Portugal / "Zürcher Theater Spektakel," Theater Werft, Zürich, Switzerland / "het pact," de warande stad turnhout, Turnhout, Belgium / "BITE 98," Barbican Centre, London, UK / Kampnagel Theater, Hamburg, Germany / Dansens Hus, Stockholm, Sweden

LOVE/SEX/DEATH/MONEY/LIFE | installation | in the exhibition "Donai yanen! Et maintenant! La création contemporain au Japon," École nationale supérieure des beaux-arts, Paris, France

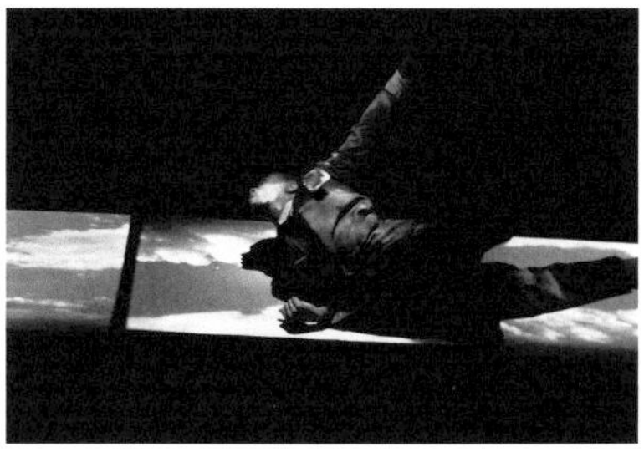

pH

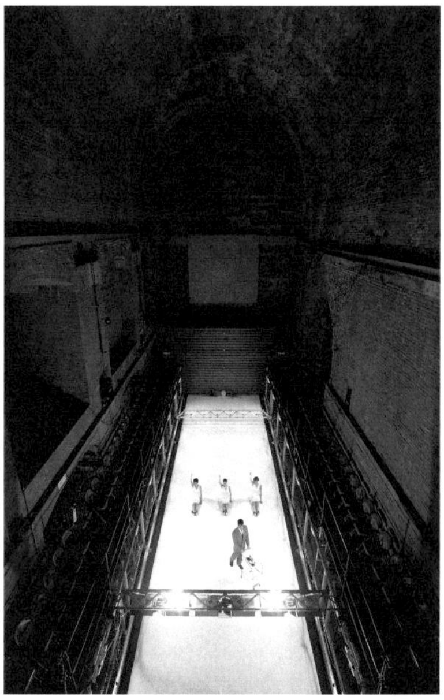

pH

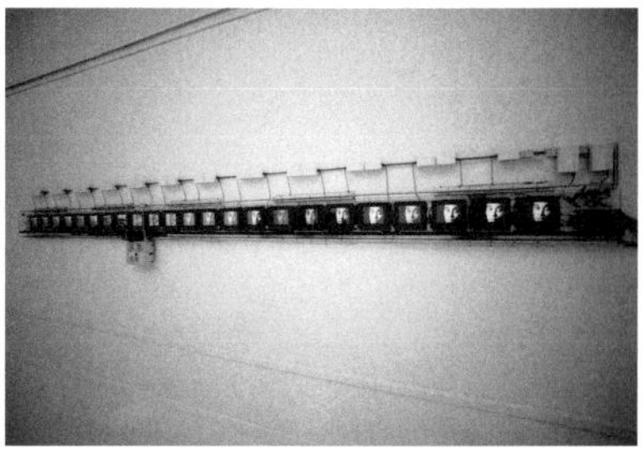

S/N #1

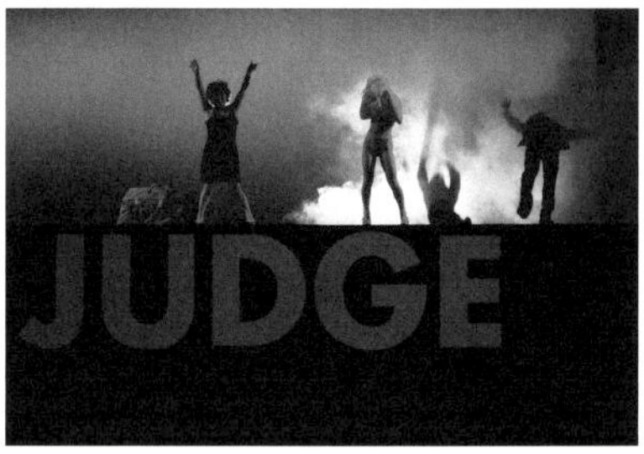

S/N

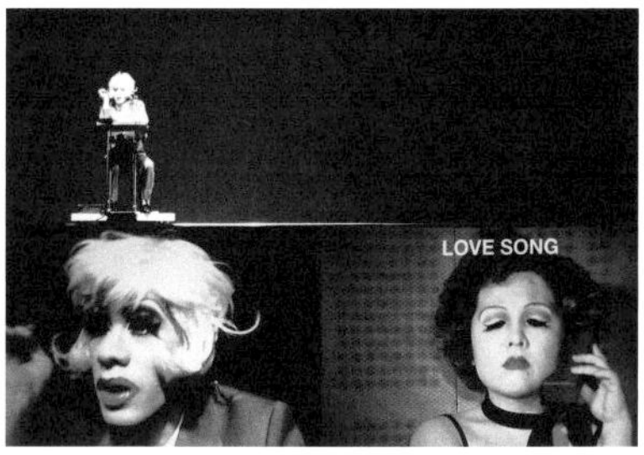

S/N

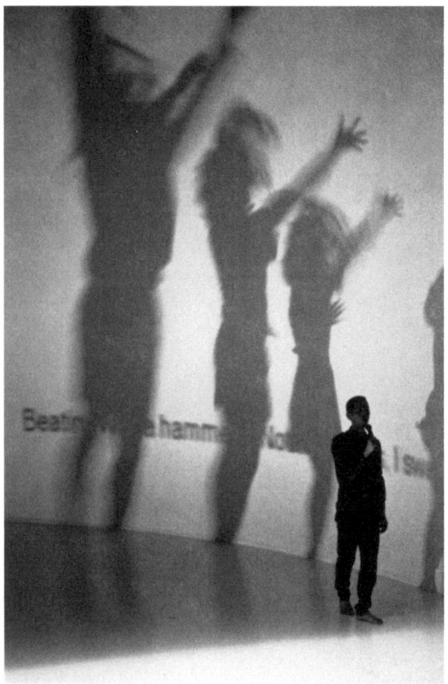

OR

1999 **Sweet Memories** | working title, performance, public rehearsal | "Festival Studio Vidéo Danse," Théâtre Kallisté, Ajaccio, Corsica, France
OR | performance | The Museum of Art, Kochi, Japan / "Kyoto Arts Festival," Kyoto City North Culture Hall, Kyoto, Japan / "Donaufestival," Theaterhaus Alte Sporthalle, Krems, Austria / On The Boards, Seattle, USA / PICA (Portland Institute for Contemporary Art), Portland, USA / Walker Art Center, Minneapolis, USA / Museum of Contemporary Art, Chicago, USA
LOVE/SEX/DEATH/MONEY/LIFE | installation | in the exhibition "Fancy Dance," Artsonje Museum, Kyongju, Korea / Artsonje Center, Seoul, Korea
memorandum | performance | "Festival de danse," Le Manège Scène Nationale, Espace Gérard Philipe, Maubeuge, France / "Festival d'Automne à Paris," Maison des Arts de Créteil, Créteil, France / Haus der Kulturen der Welt, Arena, Berlin, Germany / "Festival de Otoño," YSARCA, Teatro Albeniz, Madrid, Spain

2000 **OR** | installation | in the exhibition "Musiques en Scène," Musée d'Art Contemporain de Lyon (permanent collection), Lyon, France / "Gendai: Japanese Contemporary Art—Between the Body and Space," Centre for Contemporary Art Ujazdowski Castle, Warsaw, Poland
memorandum | performance | "Charleroi Danse," Charleroi, Belgium / GRAME + Maison de la Danse, Lyon, France / Centre de Développement Chorégraphique + TNT/Théâtre de la Cité, Toulouse, France / Teatro Central, Sevilla, Spain / "Julidans," Stadsschouwburg, Amsterdam, The Netherlands / "tanz aus japan: international sommerfestival 2000," Tanzhaus NRW, Düsseldorf, Germany / "La Bâtie Festival de Genève," Bâtiment des Forces Motrices, Genève, Switzerland / The Museum of Art, Kochi, Japan / New National Theatre, Tokyo, Japan / Theater Drama City, Osaka, Japan
cascade | installation & performance | in the exhibition "Stanze e Segreti," Salone del Mobile, Milano, Italy
LOVE/SEX/DEATH/MONEY/LIFE | installation | in the exhibition "vision.ruhr," Museum am Ostwall, Dortmund, Germany

2001 **cascade** | installation & performance | in the exhibition "Translated Acts: Performance and Body Art from East Asia," Haus der Kulturen der Welt, Berlin, Germany

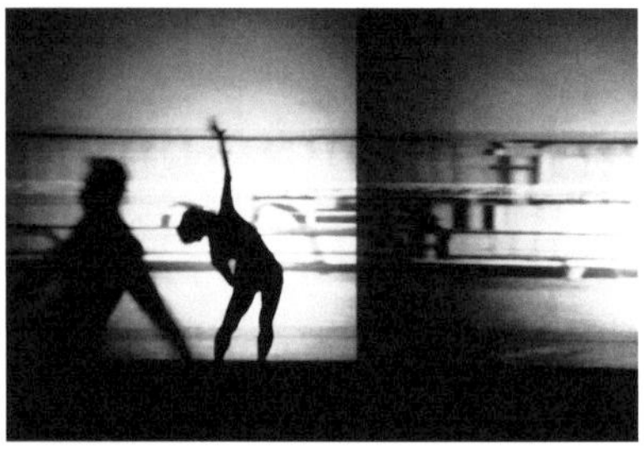

memorandum

2002 **memorandum** | performance | New Opera of Tel Aviv, Tel Aviv, Israel / Museum of Contemporary Art, Chicago, USA / On The Boards, Seattle, USA / PICA (Portland Institute for Contemporary Art), Newmark Theater, Portland, USA / Walker Art Center, Minneapolis, USA / "Festival ART ROCK," La Passerelle, St. Brieuc, France / Maison des Arts de Créteil, Créteil, France / "Singapore Arts Festival," Victoria Theatre, Singapore / Istana Budaya, The Japan Foundation Kuala Lumpur, Kuala Lumpur, Malaysia
OR | installation | École supérieure des beaux-arts, Toulouse, France
Voyage | performance | Centre de Développment Chorégraphique de Toulouse/Midi-Pyrénées + TNT/Théâtre de la Cité, Toulouse, France / Le Parvis Scène Nationale, Ibos-Tarbes, France / Saitama Arts Theater, Saitama, Japan / Theater Drama City, Osaka, Japan / Lithuanian National Opera and Ballet Theatre, Vilnius, Lithuania / Vanemuine Theatre, Tartu, Estonia / Latvijas Nacionala Opera, Riga, Latvia / Le-Maillon Théâtre de Strasbourg, Strasbourg, France
Voyages | installation | NTT InterCommunication Center [ICC], Tokyo, Japan

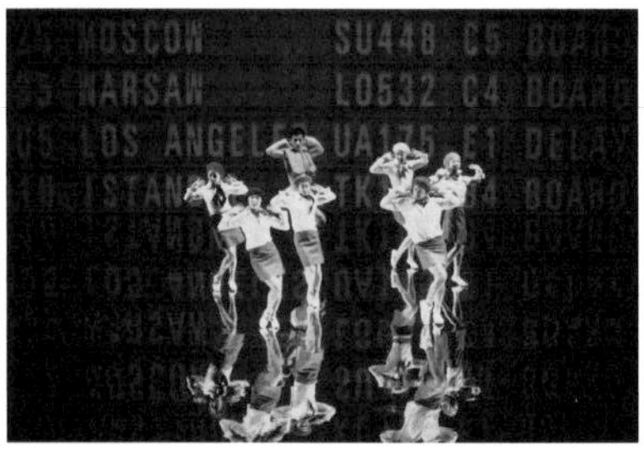

Voyage

2003 **Voyage** | performance | Deutsches Nationaltheater und Staatskapelle Weimar, Weimar, Germany / Biwako Hall Center for the Performing Arts, Shiga, Japan / REDCAT (Roy and Edna Disney/CalArts Theater), Los Angeles, USA / Maison des Arts de Créteil, Créteil, France
memorandum | performance | "The 22nd International Modern Dance Festival," The KCAF Arts Theater, Seoul, Korea / "La Biennale di Venezia," Teatro Piccolo Arsenale, Venice, Italy / Bangkok Playhouse, Bangkok, Thailand / "Melbourne International Arts Festival," Forum Theatre, Melbourne, Australia / REDCAT (Roy and Edna Disney/CalArts Theater), Los Angeles, USA / Pittsburgh Dance Council, Pittsburgh, USA
OR | installation | in the exhibition "Cinémas du futur," Lille 2004—Capitale européenne de la culture Euralille, Lille, France

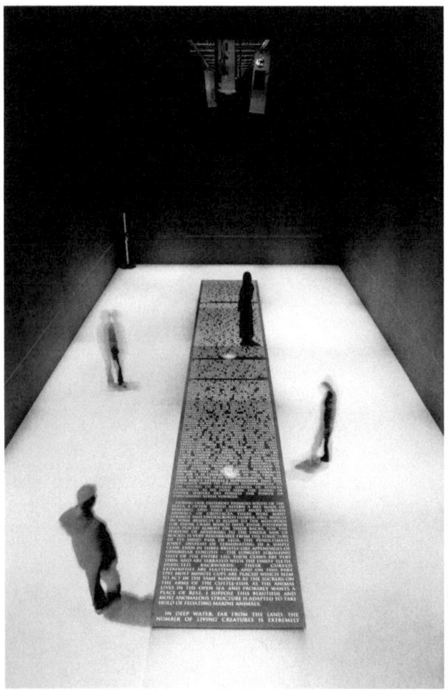

Voyages

2004 **Voyages** | installation | Yamaguchi Center for Arts and Media [YCAM], Yamaguchi, Japan
Voyage | performance | Yamaguchi Center for Arts and Media [YCAM], Yamaguchi, Japan / Novel Hall for Performing Arts, Taipei, Taiwan / "Tanztheater 3 wochen mit Pina Bausch," Schauspielhaus, Düsseldorf, Germany

2005 **Voyage** | performance | Théâtre d'Angoulême, Angoulême, France / Le Carré des Jalles, St Médard en Jalles, France / Dansens Hus, Stockholm, Sweden / "Bergen International Festival," Bergen, Norway / "International Modern Dance Festival," The KCAF Arts Theater, Seoul, Korea / Muffathalle, München, Germany / Altstadherbst Kulturfestival Düsseldorf, Düsseldorf, Germany
OR | installation | TESLA BERLIN, Berlin, Germany

2006 **Voyage** | performance | La Comète Scène Nationale de Châlons-en-Champagne, Châlons-en-Champagne, France / Théâtre de Nîmes, Nîmes, France / Posthof, Linz, Austria / Tramway, Glasgow, UK / "Exodos Festival," Cankarjev Dom, Ljubljana, Slovenia / "Melbourne International Arts Festival," Playhouse Theatre, Melbourne, Australia

2007 **Voyages** | installation | in the exhibition "Body Media," Shanghai Sculpture Space, 0 ART CENTER, Shanghai Institute of Visual Art Fudan University, Shanghai, China / "NAMURA ART MEETING '04–'34," Studio Partita, Osaka, Japan / "Vom Funken zum Pixel," Martin-Gropius-Bau, Berlin, Germany

2008 **Voyage** | performance | "XI FESTIVAL IBEROAMERICANO DE TEATRO DE BOGOTA," Bogota, Colombia / EMPAC (Experimental Media & Performing Arts Center), Rensselaer Polytechnic Institute, Troy, NY, USA / Montclair State University, Alexander Kasser Theater, Montclair, NJ, USA / LA FILATURE, Mulhouse, France / LE VOLCAN—Scène Nationale du Havre, Le Havre, France
S/N | performance documentary screening | NTT InterCommunication Center [ICC], Tokyo, Japan

2009 **Voyage** | performance | O.M.M.A. (Organismos Megarou Mousikis Athinon) The Athens Concert Hall, Athens, Greece / SEMEC (Societe d'Economie Mixte pour les Evenements Cannois), Palais des Festivals et des Congrès, Theatre Debussy, Cannes, France
OR, memorandum | DVD | released by commmons, Tokyo, Japan

2010 **S/N** | performance documentary screening | in the exhibition "Roppongi Crossing 2010: Can There Be Art?" Mori Art Museum, Tokyo, Japan
pH, S/N, OR, memorandum, Voyage | performance documentary screening | NTT InterCommunication Center [ICC], Tokyo, Japan
LOVE/SEX/DEATH/MONEY/LIFE | installation | in the exhibition "LIFE with ART," Kyoto Seika University Gallery Fleur, Kyoto, Japan

2012 **pH** | video | "Double Vision: contemporary art from Japan," Moscow Museum of Modern Art, Moscow, Russia

2013 **pH, S/N, OR** | performance documentary screening | in the exhibition "Re: Quest—Japanese Contemporary Art since the 1970s," Seoul National University Museum of Art, Seoul, Korea

2014 **MEMORANDUM OR VOYAGE** | installation | in the exhibition "Seeking New Genealogies—Bodies / Leaps / Traces," Museum of Contemporary Art, Tokyo, Japan
memorandum | performance documentary screening | in the exhibition "Code Act," Coreana Museum of Art, Space*C, Seoul, Korea

2017 **MEMORANDUM OR VOYAGE** | installation | in the exhibition "Reenacting History: Collective Actions and Everyday Gestures," National Museum of Modern and Contemporary Art, Gwacheon, Korea / "ROMAEUROPA DIGITALIFE," Palazzo delle Esposizioni, Rome, Italy
MEMORANDUM OR VOYAGE | installation | Centre Pompidou, France (permanent collection)

2018 **DUMB TYPE | ACTIONS + RÉFLEXIONS** | solo exhibition | Centre Pompidou-Metz, Metz, France
pH, S/N | performance documentary special screening | "YCC Temporary," YCC Yokohama Creativecity Center, Kanagawa, Japan

2019 **DUMB TYPE New Project—work in progress** | public rehearsal | ROHM Theatre Kyoto, Kyoto, Japan
DUMB TYPE | ACTIONS + REFLECTIONS | solo exhibition | Museum of Contemporary Art, Tokyo, Japan

2020 **2020** | performance | ROHM Theatre Kyoto, Kyoto, Japan [cancelled due to Covid-19 pandemic]
2020 | performance documentary, film screening | ROHM Theatre Kyoto, Kyoto, Japan

2022 **2022** | installation | The 59th International Art Exhibition – La Biennale di Venezia, The Japan Pavilion, Venice, Italy
DUMB TYPE | solo exhibition | Haus der Kunst, Munich, Germany

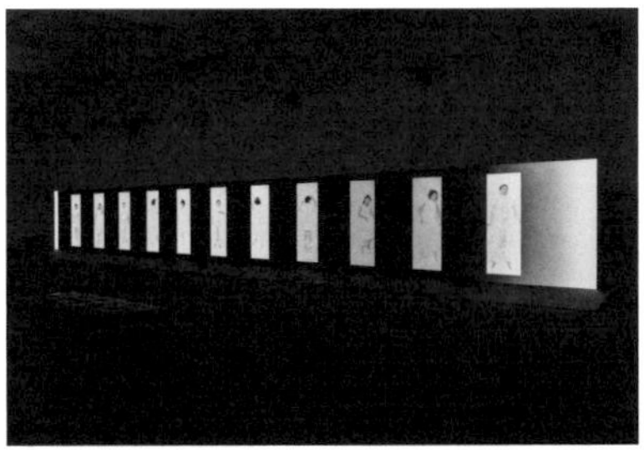
MEMORANDUM OR VOYAGE

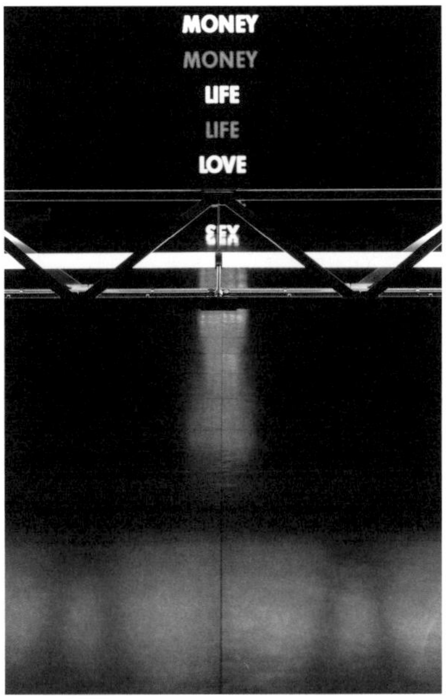

pH (front) | LOVE/SEX/DEATH/MONEY/LIFE (back)

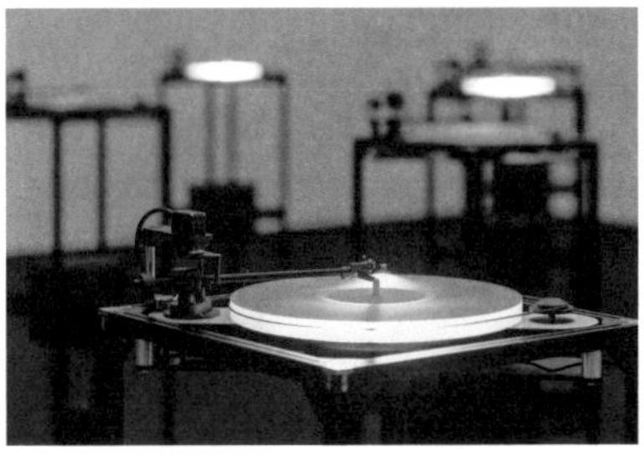
Playback

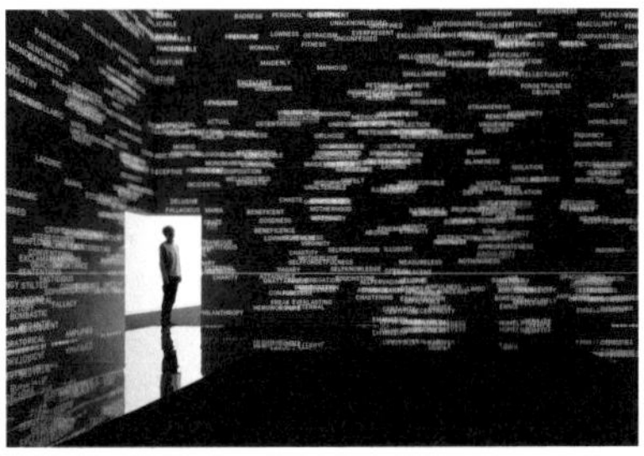
TRACE/REACT II

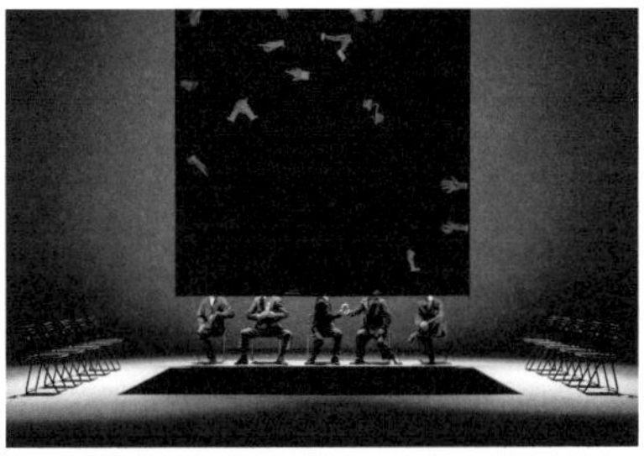
2020

ダムタイプ｜2022
第59回ヴェネチア・ビエンナーレ国際美術展　日本館
2022年4月23日–11月27日

アーティスト：ダムタイプ

コミッショナー：国際交流基金
伊東正伸
牧瀬浩一
鈴木達也
三輪桃子
鶴井百合奈
マリア・クリスティーナ・ガスペリーニ

現地コーディネーター：
武藤春美

現地技術スタッフ：
ヴァレンティノ・パスコロ
ヤコポ・ダヴィド

特別助成：公益財団法人 石橋財団

Dumb Type, *2022*
The 59th International Art Exhibition – La Biennale di Venezia,
The Japan Pavilion
23 April–27 November 2022

Artist: Dumb Type

Commissioner: The Japan Foundation
Masanobu Ito
Koichi Makise
Tatsuya Suzuki
Momoko Miwa
Yurina Tsurui Oue
Maria Cristina Gasperini

Local coordinator:
Harumi Muto

Local technician:
Valentino Pascolo
Jacopo David

With special support of:
Ishibashi Foundation

ダムタイプ
2022

発行日：2023年2月25日　初版第一刷

企画：国際交流基金、ダムタイプ
編集：高谷桜子（ダムタイプ）、鈴木達也（国際交流基金）

写真：
高谷史郎［p.5, pp.11–21, p.23, pp.24–25（下）, pp.26–29, pp.31–32］
世利之［p.22, pp.24–25（上）, p.30］

年譜図版［pp.64–71］中林正巳、福永一夫、高谷史郎、高谷桜子、Arno Declair、大高隆、椎木静寧、表恒匡、Emmanuel Valette、井上嘉和

デザイン：南 琢也
翻訳：空 音央、水野 響［pp.44–47］
編集協力・制作：望月かおる（美術出版社）、今野綾花
印刷・製本：株式会社サンエムカラー

発行人：山下和樹
発行：カルチュア・コンビニエンス・クラブ株式会社
　　株式会社美術出版社書籍編集部
発売：株式会社美術出版社
〒141-8203　東京都品川区上大崎 3-1-1
目黒セントラルスクエア5F
電話：03-6809-0318（代表）　03-5280-7442（編集）
https://www.bijutsu.press

Printed in Japan

ISBN 978-4-568-10550-6 C3070

DUMB TYPE
2022

Published on November 10th, 2022

Produced by the Japan Foundation and Dumb Type
Edited by Yoko Takatani (Dumb Type),
Tatsuya Suzuki (Japan Foundation)

Photography:
Shiro Takatani (p.5, pp.11–21, p.23, pp.24–25 [bottom], pp.26–29, pp.31–32),
Yuki Seli (p.22, pp.24–25 [above], p.30)

Photos in the chronicle pages (pp.64–71)
Masami Nakabayashi, Kazuo Fukunaga,
Shiro Takatani, Yoko Takatani, Arno Declair,
Takashi Ohtaka, Shizune Shiigi, Nobutada Omote,
Emmanuel Valette, Yoshikazu Inoue

Catalogue Design: Takuya Minami
Translation: Neo Sora, Hibiki Mizuno (pp.44–47)
Catalogue Edit and Coordination:
Kaoru Mochizuki (Bijutsu Shuppan-sha), Ayaka Konno
Printing and Binding: SunM Color Co., Ltd.

Publisher: Kazuki Yamashita
Published by Culture Convenience Club Co., Ltd.
Sale by Bijutsu Shuppan-sha Co., Ltd.
5F, Meguro Central Square, 3-1-1
Kamiosaki, Shinagawa-ku, Tokyo 141-8203 JAPAN
Tel: +81-3-6809-0318
https://www.bijutsu.press